KU-184-051

TWO CENTURIES OF Irish history

BASED ON
A BBC RADIO SERIES
EDITED BY
JAMES HAWTHORNE

BRITISH
BROADCASTING
CORPORATION

Published by the British Broadcasting Corporation
35 Marylebone High Street, London, W1M 4AA
© British Broadcasting Corporation 1966
First published 1966
Reprinted 1967, 1969
Revised edition 1974

ACKNOWLEDGEMENTS

Acknowledgement is due to the following for permission to reproduce illustrations

ANVIL BOOKS Black and Tans, page 71

BELFAST TELEGRAPH O'Neill and Lemass, page 74

CENTRAL PRESS PHOTOS LTD Carson inspecting, page 68

F. CZIRA Howth gun-running, page 69

'GAEL-LINN' John Redmond, page 66, gun-running, page 68

GOVERNMENT INFORMATION SERVICE State opening of Parliament, page 74

INDEPENDENT NEWSPAPERS LTD Collins and de Valera, page 70, British troops, page 73

BRENDAN KEOGH Citizen Army, page 66, Easter Rising, page 69

LINEN HALL LIBRARY Battle of Antrim from *Ulster Journal of Archaeology*, front and back cover and page 60

THE MANSELL COLLECTION 'King' O'Connell, page 61, Gladstone, page 64

NATIONAL GALLERY OF IRELAND Wolfe Tone, page 60

NATIONAL LIBRARY OF IRELAND Irish Parliament, page 59, famine, roll-call, page 62, Parnell leaving House of Commons, page 63, eviction, page 64, volunteers poster, page 106, proclamation, page 111

RADIO TIMES HULTON PICTURE LIBRARY Daniel O'Connell, page 61, attack on van, page 63, Carson, page 67, Peace Agreement, page 72, Covenant, page 101

ULSTER MUSEUM volunteers parading, page 59, poster, page 65

UNITED NATIONS Mr Boland and Mr Aiken, page 73.

Printed in England by
The Broadwater Press Ltd, Welwyn Garden City, Hertfordshire
ISBN 0 563 10913 0

Stockton - Billingham
LIBRARY
Technical College

28841

941.5

CONTENTS

EDITOR'S NOTE

'TWO CENTURIES OF IRISH HISTORY' was first broadcast in the Northern Ireland Home Service in the Spring of 1965 as a series of eleven weekly broadcasts. It was intended primarily for the 14–15 age group in secondary schools within the Province and, broadly speaking, its aim was to make clearer the events that led to the creation of Northern Ireland.

Northern Ireland is often held to be a history-conscious community and yet the man-in-the-street – and certainly his teenage son or daughter at the secondary school – knows very little about the origins of that small six-county political unit which was created less than half a century ago. The reasons for this situation are complex, but the one that is most frequently suggested is that the Ulsterman, whether he is descended from the indigenous Celt or the British planter, is willing only to look back selectively at the past. A total view of history might erode that pride in his ancestry which determines his attitude to the community and especially to those members of it who – to use an Ulster phrase – 'dig with the other foot'. Indeed, for several generations the formal teaching of local history has been largely neglected. My own view is that the Ulsterman is seldom embarrassed by history, however distasteful, provided he is sure that what he is being told is the truth. With typically northern caution he will examine the credentials of the historian and if he finds that his ethnic origins are sound then will his scholarship be also. This practice aggravates the already chronic shortage of popular history texts. A book on Northern Ireland for Northern Ireland is seldom a commercially attractive proposition for a publisher, even less so when the possible readership is halved as soon as the name of the author is disclosed. Thus, all too frequently, Ulster's history is compressed into, at best, one or two semi-accurate chapters in a book covering, say, the whole of Britain or Ireland.

Happily the BBC enjoys a reputation for impartiality, and so when the series began last January it received immediate acclaim from the press. Newspapers all over Ireland carried reports, at least two ran leading articles. Some editors gave it headlines – 'Radio History', 'Revolution in Radio', 'New Light on Ireland' – and one correspondent wrote: 'If the meeting [the historic meeting between Mr O'Neill and Mr Lemass] was the beginning of a great advance in economic relations in Ireland, the BBC's new history series for schools is an equally great advance in education.' That the series *has* been an advance we cannot lay claim but it was certainly well received by schools and by the public at large and it has been this favourable reception which, I know, led Mr Robert McCall, Controller Northern Ireland, to ask me to prepare this publication. This of course is not the first history book to be produced from broadcasts in the Northern Ireland Home Service. In the 1950s two volumes entitled *Ulster since 1800* emerged from a series of talks; indeed it has been the success of these books which leads us to hope that *Two Centuries of Irish History* will be an equally useful aid in schools and colleges. We should also hope that those whose schooldays are irretrievably gone will find the book interesting too; many of that number who were in a position to eavesdrop on Monday mornings to the schools programmes were pleased with what they heard and some were kind enough to write and tell us so.

As a short history of Ireland this little book is somewhat unconventional. Had each contributor been asked to write primarily for publication in book form he would doubtless have approached his task in a very different way. Writing for radio is a specialized art with its own disciplines but, on the other hand, with its own rewards. A schools' audience imposes further restriction, but again, it offers greater scope in other ways. Each of the eleven chapters of this book was designed to be a twenty-minute aural assault on the routine of the classroom. The presentation was lively and dramatic with actors bringing to life the words that in the book are mere documentary evidence. Music was also important and, where appropriate, background effects; in the book, the effects have disappeared and the songs and ballads are represented only by italics. But if the printed page has reduced the effect of the writing then, conversely, teachers may use the book as a script from which pupils can re-create a broadcast of their own.

The greatest problem with the whole series was, of course, not with the presentation of the history but with the history itself. The aim of 'making clearer the events that led to the creation of Northern Ireland' – as the N.I. Sub-Committee of the Schools Broadcasting Council put it – is not easy to realize. Suppose one accepts that Northern Ireland came into existence because of *unionist* determination. How can this determination be explained and why did it succeed? When did unionism begin to grow? Was unionism not a reaction to *nationalism* and nationalism a reaction to conquest in one form or another? Thus, even before the fundamental issues are examined, one is concerned with Strongbow and the Anglo-Norman adventurers of the twelfth century. Obviously in a series of eleven broadcasts it would be impracticable to start so far back; and yet it would be improper to begin at some point in modern history which would ignore any of the grievances or aspirations that produced the turmoil of the 1920s and the partitioning of Ireland. Having taken into account as many as possible of these factors it seemed appropriate to start with a programme describing the social and political conditions of Ireland in the late eighteenth century and then to follow with a programme dealing specifically with the insurrection of 1798, a rebellion which had not only special relevance to Ulster but which was the immediate cause of the Act which united Ireland constitutionally with Great Britain. From then on it was felt that the path of Ireland's troubled history should be traced throughout the nineteenth century with broadcasts on the work of Daniel O'Connell, the catastrophe of the potato famine, the significance of the industrial revolution, the manœuvring of Gladstone and Parnell, leading eventually to extreme separatist nationalism in the Fenian and Sinn Fein traditions. From there the series would deal in slightly greater detail with the events of the twentieth century – the Ulster crisis of 1910–13, the 1916 rebellion and the troubles of 1920–2. A final programme was to examine the problems facing the newly-created Northern Ireland.

No series on Irish history would have succeeded if listeners had not had the fullest confidence in the impartiality and authority of the writing. I was particularly happy that the writers I had in mind for the series – writers whom I knew were possessed of all the necessary skill and scholarship for such a task – were all able to accept my invitation. Add to this the fact that three leading authorities on Irish history were invited to vet every single script and to advise in the planning of the series as a whole and in the writing of the teachers' notes and pupils' pamphlets. They were Professor J. C. Beckett of Queen's University Belfast, Professor G. A. Hayes-McCoy of University College Galway, and Professor J. L. McCracken of Magee University College Londonderry; to these three the scriptwriters and I are indebted. For the Spring edition of the teachers' notes Mr W. R. Hutchison of Royal School Dungannon wrote the historical summary and this has been incorporated as a general introduction to this book. In the preparation of the Autumn edition of the notes, extracts of which are being used to introduce each chapter, I had most helpful advice from Mr Douglas Carson of Orangefield Boys' Secondary School. My colleague Mr David Hammond did invaluable research into the songs and ballads and I am also grateful to museum and library officials in Ireland and England – too numerous to mention – for their energy and goodwill in helping me to trace documents and illustrations. Finally, the BBC is indebted to its listeners, especially those in the teaching profession. The evaluation of the classroom is of paramount importance to the makers of school broadcasts and so, in the light of the many useful comments on the Spring series, the scripts for the Autumn repeat were amended here and there to increase the effectiveness of the programmes as a teaching aid. This revised version, in which listeners have had a part to play, is the one which is now offered as a permanent printed record.

James Hawthorne, Broadcasting House, Belfast 2.
1966

BACKGROUND NOTES

First published in
TWO CENTURIES OF IRISH HISTORY
Notes for the Teacher leaflet Spring 1965

W. R. Hutchison

LATE EIGHTEENTH-CENTURY IRELAND

THE CHOICE of the second half of the eighteenth century as a starting point for this series of broadcasts is particularly happy. That age compares with the present in many respects. Throughout Western Europe it was the age of reason. The softening of the harshness of the Irish Penal Code was a reflection of a growing tolerance in religious and political matters in France and other European countries. Commercial rivalries began to replace doctrinal bigotries as motives for war. It would of course be quite wrong to assume that the welfare state was an aim of any significant group of eighteenth-century thinkers, or that social and religious discrimination was about to disappear, but there were definite signs that the foundations of the *establishment* in Ireland, as elsewhere, were beginning to crack. Reference has been made to the growth of commercial rivalries. The second half of the eighteenth century saw the rapid expansion of Irish industry and commerce, and the introduction of greatly improved farming methods. This meant increased wealth in the hands of a new and strong middle class. But it was a middle class which was largely excluded from full civil and political equality with the traditionally privileged order of the landed gentry, and this led to a more active and effective discontent than ever before. Though the land had become more productive, the new foundations of wealth – at least in the north – were in the linen industry, and, as the century progressed, this tended to concentrate more and more in the north. Belfast began to replace Dublin as the main centre, and while Dublin remained the seat of government and arbiter of taste, it was for very good reasons that her commercial rival earned the title, 'Athens of the North'.

Since the Jacobean Plantation (in 1609) Ulster had acquired a character more distinct from that of the three other provinces of Ireland than any differences which separated those three provinces from one another. Towards the end of the eighteenth century this character had become even more individual. Throughout Ireland as a whole the conditions under which the peasant farmer earned his living were deplorable. The *Whiteboy* movement expressed his discontent in the south as the *Oakboys* and *Hearts of Steel* expressed it in the north. But in Ulster, *Tenant Right* gave special privileges to farmers, i.e. security of tenure, provided rents were paid, and some compensation for improvements. This enabled them to look to the future with a greater degree of hope than their less fortunate brethren in the south. In the 1780s Grattan's Parliament achieved a measure of independence from the English. But it had never entertained republican ideas. The link with the English Crown remained the chief ingredient of its political thinking. It was different in northern political circles. Until the 1780s northern Protestants had looked to England as their natural ally and protector. Now, Ulster whiggery, closely associated with the growth of the linen industry, gave the Parliament at Westminster grave cause for anxiety.

THE UNITED IRISHMEN. This brings us to the '98, the first rebellion in which Irish Protestants took up arms against the British Government. It did not originate in Ulster. Its seeds had been sown by Charlemont, Grattan, Flood and other Irish patriots when, in the 1780s, they called on the Volunteers, at first a purely military organization, to back up their claims to political independence. What began as an attack on one kind of establishment (the English) by another (the Irish), ended as an attempt to abolish prescriptive right in whatever quarter under whatever disguise it might be found. Irish landlords were the pillars of the Established Church, the custodians of property, engrossers of office, but they had resented having to share all these good things with Englishmen. Resistance once aroused, however, and the wishes of the landlords having in good measure been met, the control of events began to pass into the hands of the vast substratum of the underprivileged peasantry, domestic linen weavers and merchants.

The Society of United Irishmen embodied the aspirations of a large proportion of these people. Organized chiefly by Wolfe Tone, it had a new and formidable programme: nothing less than the grant of full civil and political rights, equality before the law, abolition of religious discrimination, equality of opportunity, together with the purging of political life of the corrupt practices which had bedevilled it throughout the eighteenth century. Some of these reforms had been advocated in the Irish Parliament, but when the United Irishman movement became militant the Irish landlords found themselves in much greater sympathy with their English cousins than with their own tenants and the industrial proletariat.

The United men were driven into open rebellion not only by their longstanding grievances and by the banning of their organization, but also by the brutality of the military whose preventive excesses gave some foretaste of twentieth-century Nazism. They were tempted into it by the offers of French help. French revolutionary ideas had inspired them – especially in the north – and now that France was at war with Britain the opportunity to use French troops seemed too good to be refused.

As it happened, French help proved as much an embarrassment as an advantage to the United cause. In the first place, it emphasized the differences which lay embedded in the apparent unity of the rebels. The peasantry of the south were interested primarily in relief from appalling conditions of land tenure, the more industrialized north were primarily inspired by French republicanism. Military leadership, when the rebellion broke out, was amateurish and unco-ordinated. In short, it never had a chance of success – without French help.

DANIEL O'CONNELL. When it was finally put down the English Prime Minister, Pitt, was confirmed in his view that the only permanent solution to Ireland's problems was union with Great Britain. If a mere 100 Irish members were allowed seats at Westminster, dangerous enthusiasms could be effectively curbed, and trading anomalies solved. When, in 1801, the Act came into force, Ireland's brief period of parliamentary independence and her

7

opportunity to achieve full civil rights and religious equality ended. When O'Connell heard the news he wished for any alternative – even the return of the Penal Code, if only the Parliament in College Square could be re-established. The role of leader which now fell to his lot was a new one for an Irish Catholic gentleman. There had, of course, been Catholic soldiers of genius, and they had done much to shape the course of Irish history, but those who had effectively mobilized and directed public opinion had (for the most part) been Protestants. Swift, Grattan, Tone – all had belonged to that fold. But here was a Catholic Irishman who spoke the Irish language (though privately he considered it too primitive to suit modern needs) and who could thus win support from a wider and deeper stratum of opinion than any of his predecessors. He believed in the power of persuasion rather than in force to achieve his ends, reserving the possibility of force as an added persuasion. To the Catholic masses he was 'the Liberator'. But his leadership, though powerful, placed the Ulster Protestant community in something of a dilemma. The Orange Order, founded in 1795, was attracting to its ranks support from established and dissenting churches alike. With the defeat of Napoleon in 1815 and the return of the exiled Bourbons to the French throne the moral support for Ulster republicanism disappeared. There was less enthusiasm than formerly for Catholic emancipation.

Catholic emancipation had been one of the objectives of the United Irishmen. O'Connell made it his first aim. Further, if Catholics could have the right to sit in Parliament, he reasoned, the constitutional path to repeal of the Act of Union would be open. He decided to stand as a candidate at the next general election himself. The Clare election campaign of 1829 made history, not only as being the first to use the technique of open air meetings and highly organized propaganda, but because it had as its object the choice of a parliamentary candidate who, by existing law, was disqualified from holding a seat. Thanks to the personality of O'Connell and the enthusiasm of his supporters – to the very real danger of violence – and to the statesmanship of the Wellesley brothers, one of whom was Prime Minister at the time and one Lord Lieutenant (both, as experienced soldiers, well versed in the implications of war) all obstacles were overcome and the first Catholic Irishman ever to sit in the Union Parliament took his seat. (No Catholic had held a seat in an Irish Parliament since 1689.) Emancipation marked the disappearance of the last of the Penal Laws. Catholics were now in full possession of civil rights and could look forward with confidence to the removal of land grievances and recognition of their church as the real church of Ireland.

It seemed iniquitous to O'Connell (and to many Protestants) that the Established Church, with its minority membership, should draw financial support from the non-church majority. By law tithes were payable to it by churchmen, Catholic and Dissenter alike. O'Connell's efforts to remove this grievance were, however, only partially successful. The Tithe Commutation Act of 1838 did not abolish the tax which was now transferred to the already burdened shoulders of the farmer, but at least it provided a soothing disguise and it paved the way for Gladstone's Irish Church Disestablishment Act of 1869.

So far Ulster Dissenters had, on the whole, been with O'Connell. They could not very well oppose the Emancipation of Catholics when they themselves had received a similar privilege (as they did in 1828). How could they deplore the removal or disguise of tithes? But when O'Connell's main aim, repeal of the Union, became apparent the majority felt they could no longer maintain their role as fellow-travellers. When the Liberator invited Ulster to mobilize support for his Repeal campaign, he met with strong opposition, mainly from the Presbyterians under the leadership of Dr Cooke, and he had to return to Dublin with empty hands. By this time Ulster dissent had accepted the Union and were increasingly anxious about the effects of the subsequent Catholic revival on their own security. O'Connell's downfall came when, true to his principles of non-violence, he accepted Peel's ban of a monster demonstration he had arranged to take place at Clontarf in 1843. He was arrested and, in spite of his popularity among opposition members in the House of Commons, confined to prison. The majority of his followers diverted their allegiance to the Young Ireland organization which, with its belief in physical force, had already split the Repeal movement.

THE FAMINE. One of the factors which contributed to the failure of both O'Connell and the Young Irelanders was the Great Famine of 1845 (and those of the five following years). As the potato was the cheapest and most prolific form of agricultural produce it had become the sole diet of practically the entire peasant population. When blight reached Ireland from America in 1845 it therefore threatened complete disaster. Though the worst was avoided in 1845, when there was only a partial failure of the crop, there was no escape in the following year when three-quarters of it was destroyed. The reaction of private individuals and organizations in Ireland, England and America was immediate. Charity poured in from these sources in volume. Queen Victoria decreed a day of prayer for the victims. But these admirable acts concealed deeper issues. The Union was still in force. Many Irishmen believed that the famine disaster was a proof of the Government's failure to govern Ireland. When O'Connell proposed that the ports should be closed to the export of food from Ireland, the British Government refused to agree. To have done so might not have been an effective remedy but it would at least have been a gesture of goodwill. If Britain, influenced as she was by the principles of *laissez-faire* and Free Trade, refused to accept responsibility for the social welfare of an outlying territory, the inhabitants of that territory could be forgiven for regarding self-help and self-determination as highly moral aims. Thus the famine gave renewed stimulus to the demand for Home Rule.

THE FENIANS. This stimulus was embodied in the Fenian movement which originated with Irish famine refugees in America and was maintained by the constant flow of emigrants in the years following the famine. At home, many landlords had been ruined by the stoppage of rents and had been forced to sell their estates. Parliament passed the Encumbered Estates Act to facilitate the transfer to the new owners who, it was hoped, would live on their premises and do something to make Irish farming a more economic proposition than it had been in the past. Unfortunately the new estate owners proved to be expert at turning the screw on their tenants, but at very little else. Absenteeism became, if anything, worse than before. Farms required capital for development but the peasants had none to use and the landlords drained away whatever they could raise in rent to spend in England. Thus the way was paved for fifty years of agrarian unrest and increasingly savage repression; hence evictions, the continued flow of emigrants to the

United States and Britain and the intensity of the Home Rule struggle in the age of Gladstone and Parnell. Ulster, chiefly because of the benefits of Tenant Right and the prosperity of her linen industry, suffered less from the famine than other parts of the country. So it was that the tidal flow of emigration to America, unlike that of the previous century, was mainly of southern origin.

INDUSTRIAL REVOLUTION. It was in Ulster too that the full impact of the Industrial Revolution was felt. As most of the linen was woven in Ulster farmhouses, so it was in Ulster, about the middle of the century, that most of the steam-driven machinery was set up. The Lagan Valley became the centre of the industrial Black North. New factories and shipyards made heavy demands on manpower and, while populations in the more distant counties shrank, they increased rapidly in Belfast and in the near-by industrial areas. In 1800 the city numbered 20,000 inhabitants; in 1850, 100,000. In 1858 the Belfast works of Messrs Hickson, covering a mere $3\frac{1}{2}$ acres, were taken over by Edmund J. Harland, who was joined in partnership, three years later, by G. W. Wolff. These two formed the company which was soon to bring Belfast shipyards into world prominence. Closely connected with shipbuilding was the manufacture of ropes. The Belfast Ropework Company was formed in 1873 and it expanded in step with its mother industry. Up to 1850 only 'roll' tobacco was processed in Ireland, but in 1857 Thomas Gallagher established in Londonderry a cigarette factory whose activities he transferred to Belfast ten years later. A large number of additional industries sprang up under the umbrella of the three leaders, which not only led to the rapid expansion of the Belfast city boundary (whose population by 1900 had reached 350,000), but stimulated activity in the surrounding countryside and in the smaller towns. Ulster was well on the way to achieving an integrated economy.

Dublin advanced less rapidly than Belfast in the industrial sphere, but it thereby escaped many of the worst evils of the Industrial Revolution. The Dublin slums were more frightful than anything that ever mushroomed in Belfast, but Dublin always had slums and these had never disfigured the city's architectural image as the monotonous rows of workers' houses disfigured Belfast. Pleasant buildings were soon engulfed in a sea of utilitarian houses and industrial premises and the Belfast panorama became characterized by chimney stacks and shipbuilding derricks. As industry expanded, cultural activity failed to keep pace. The intense excitement of Dublin literary circles in the second half of the nineteenth century and the early years of this century had no counterpart in the North. Perhaps the spur of national feeling was missing, but there was an additional cause in absorption in the pursuit of wealth.

GLADSTONE. This pursuit – and attainment – of wealth led to the strengthening of the already strong middle class which played a leading part in the moulding of public opinion in the years immediately preceding the Great War. It found itself in a somewhat uncomfortable position when Gladstone, in 1869, began the programme of Irish legislation which resulted finally in the grant of Home Rule. There was, in the beginning, much in this programme of which Ulstermen, especially the strong Presbyterian interest, could approve. It was very much to the liking of this interest that the Church should be disestablished and that something should be done (as it was in the two Land Acts) to make the farmer's life more tolerable. Besides, there was much in Gladstone's liberal philosophy, founded as it was on the principles of free enterprise and free trade, of which any industrial community could approve. But when Gladstone introduced a Home Rule Bill in 1886 many Ulstermen had second thoughts. Conditions had changed since the days of Grattan's Parliament. Then it seemed to patriots, Protestant and Catholic alike, that the future of Ireland's commercial prosperity was closely associated with an independent parliament, sitting in Dublin. Now the possibility was that Home Rule would seriously compromise Ulster's industrial relations with England, and this considerably strengthened that body of Unionist opinion which had rejected the advances of O'Connell and Young Ireland. A strong link was thus forged between unionism and commerce, a link which has lost none of its binding force down to the present day.

PARNELL. Parnell, at one stage in his career, 'The Uncrowned King of Ireland', was the driving force behind Gladstone's campaign for Home Rule. The inflexibility of his aim mobilized behind him all the nationalist groups which were working, often at cross-purposes, to the same end. He replaced Isaac Butt, leader of the Irish Party, in the House of Commons. He won the allegiance of the Land League and *Clan-na-Gael*, an Irish-American revolutionary organization, and he was even able to influence the activities of the Fenian Brotherhood whose politics were not universally acceptable in Ireland. In Parliament he perfected the technique of obstruction in order to compel a hearing of Irish problems (and so, incidentally, brought into force the *closure* or *guillotine* as a disciplinary weapon in the Speaker's hands). To Irish farmers, organized in the Land League under Michael Davitt, he recommended the pressure of boycott against unreasonable landlords, as more likely to achieve results than physical force.

'ULSTER WILL FIGHT.' Although Ulster Protestant farmers were as determined as any to secure land reform, they did not, for the most part, follow the directions of the Land League, which was much too closely associated with Home Rule for their liking. But so powerful was Parnell's influence that, in the Parliament which was elected in 1880, no fewer than 17 of the 33 Ulster seats were gained by Nationalists. When the Home Rule Bill of 1886 was introduced there was little that the sixteen Unionist M.P.s could do to stop it. But in Ulster so great was the dismay at the prospective fate of a Protestant minority in a Catholic-controlled Irish Parliament, that preparations were made to resist by force. Advertisements for the supply of 20,000 rifles and competent drill instructors appeared in Ulster newspapers.

Gladstone retired from politics for six years after his defeat, but in 1892 he returned to power as Prime Minister. Again he attempted to fulfil his ambition but by that year the celebrated divorce case in which Parnell figured had been brought to court. This ruined not only Parnell's own career but the prospect of a successful Home Rule Bill for the best part of a generation. It stiffened the resistance of non-conformists in England and Ireland alike. It brought down the thunders of the Catholic Church. For a number of years Irish nationalists, disappointed by the Parnell split, had to be content with government schemes for land purchase and with the revival of interest in the native Irish language and literature. The nationalist constitutional movement had suffered a severe blow. After the final retirement of Gladstone from public life, the Conservative Party held the upper hand at Westminster and this party had already proved itself consistently hostile to the idea of Home Rule in any form. But in 1906 the Liberals, with the support of the Irish Parliamentary Party, came back to power with an overwhelming majority. They had a programme of radical reform which included yet another Home Rule Bill for Ireland.

The Home Rule Bill of 1912 once again brought to a head all the sharp differences of opinion that had been expressed in 1886. Ulster opposition to the Bill now led by Sir Edward Carson, was organized in the Ulster Volunteer Force. On 28 September, a pledge to resist Home Rule – the celebrated 'Solemn League and Covenant' – was signed by more than 200,000 men, while the same number of women subscribed to a document associating themselves with it. Rifle clubs were formed and the drilling programme was intensified. In September an Ulster Provisional Government was nominated. When Winston Churchill, then Home Secretary in the Liberal Government at Westminster, came to Belfast to hold a Home Rule demonstration the hall selected for the meeting was seized by the Volunteers and the speeches had to be delivered in a sports field outside the city.

In the light of these and similar provocations the Westminster Government decided that the time had come to exercise discipline. A plan was drawn up to send soldiers north from the army base at the Curragh, ostensibly to provide help for the civil authorities in their maintenance of law and order, really to overawe the Volunteers. But so strong was sympathy in the Army for Ulster's dilemma that a number of the Curragh officers resigned their commissions rather than carry out the orders of the War Office. This looked dangerously like mutiny but so delicate was the situation, and so anxious was the Government to prevent an explosion that, after a short suspension, the officers were reinstated and excused. Then, on 24 April 1914, occurred the celebrated gun-running episode. The Ulster Provisional Government had purchased in Germany 50,000 rifles and three million rounds of ammunition. These were transported secretly and indirectly to Larne Harbour where, throughout the night of 24th/25th they were, with great efficiency and dispatch, distributed among groups of vehicles which had been sent to the harbour from the most distant parts of the province.

SINN FEIN, THE IRISH REPUBLICAN BROTHERHOOD AND THE LABOUR MOVEMENT. While these events were unfolding, the nationalist leader in the House of Commons was John Redmond, a man of high character and some statesmanship, but a much less dynamic figure than Parnell. He had also a much less firm grip on the allegiance of the various nationalist groups, and he had to try to come to terms with a new one – *Sinn Fein* – whose sponsor was Arthur Griffith. There were, in fact, by this time three small separatist groups at work: Sinn Fein itself, which preached the doctrine of self-reliance ('Sinn Fein' means 'We ourselves') and which saw in the Austro-Hungarian dual monarchy a possible model for a political solution in Ireland; the labour movement, which was primarily concerned with economic problems but which favoured separation, and the Irish Republican Brotherhood, descended from the Fenians, which aimed at the establishment of an Irish Republic by force. All were antagonistic to one another, all were small, almost unknown outside their own circle but they had in common a supreme contempt for Redmond and his Home Rule Bill. The labour movement had at first no particular political end in view. But when, as a direct result of a strike among Dublin transport workers and a mass demonstration in O'Connell Street which the authorities had banned, its leader, Larkin, was arrested and sentenced to seven months' imprisonment for sedition, and when, at a subsequent Board of Trade inquiry into his case, the verdict again went against him, immediate steps were taken by his followers, to form a Citizen Army with the primary object of protecting the workers, but with a view to engaging in wider political issues if the occasion should arise. About the same time the Irish Volunteers were formed by supporters of Sinn Fein as a counterblast to the Ulster Volunteers.

The example provided by Ulster on how it was possible to defy the law with impunity was not lost upon this latest organization and they, too, obtained arms from Germany. With two belligerent groups of volunteers in the country, it seemed highly probable that soon there would be armed conflict with the authorities, with the ultimate possibility of civil war. Then came the news of the assassination of the Austrian Arch-Duke, the outbreak of the European War and Britain's involvement. The warlike postures of unionists and nationalists alike gave way under the pressure of strong anti-German sentiment (perhaps more anti-German than pro-British). The Home Rule Bill, first introduced in 1912, was due to become law in September 1914, but unionist anxiety was eased by the simultaneous passage of a Bill which provided that Home Rule should be suspended for a period of twelve months, or the conclusion of the war, whichever period was of longer duration.

THE EASTER RISING. Throughout the country recruiting for the British forces went on apace; this had the support of Redmond, the Irish leader. The efforts of the left-wing nationalists to check enthusiasm failed and were condemned by the Cardinals and Bishops of the Catholic Church. A movement towards an armed revolt against British rule was now being made. But it did not get unanimous support from Irish nationalists. There were, after all, several nationalist groups with varying enthusiasms and each with its own idea as to what use should be made of the opportunity presented by Britain's involvement in the war. In 1914, Roger Casement had gone to Germany to plead the Irish case; in April 1916 he returned in a German submarine which landed him on the Kerry Coast, but he was soon taken by the police and lodged in prison. At the same time a ship carrying a cargo of arms was intercepted by a British sloop and, to avoid capture, was sunk by its own crew. Now that the expected arms were out of reach, that Casement was under arrest, that the authorities had been warned, there could be no hope at all that a rebellion would succeed. But the Irish Republican Brotherhood thought otherwise. In its view the example of sacrifice in a hopeless cause would strengthen the republican claims as nothing else could do. They decided to rise as planned. On Easter Monday, 1916, small parties of determined men seized strategic buildings in Dublin; of these the G.P.O. became the principal stronghold. Troops, including several Irish regiments, were hurried to the capital. There was sharp fighting and desperate resistance, but by the Saturday all was over. Though there were small outbreaks in counties Galway and Wexford and a more serious one in County Dublin, the main fighting took place in the city. The leaders were tried by court martial; the seven signatories of the Proclamation of the Republic, who were the Military Council of the I.R.B., and eight leaders of the Irish Volunteers and Irish Citizen Army were executed. Three months later, a like fate befell Casement.

The Easter Rising was first regarded, even by strong nationalists, as a tactical error. Many considered that it had placed Mr Redmond in a most difficult situation, at the very moment when he was about to achieve Home Rule by constitutional means, that this ideal would now have to be abandoned for at least a generation. Besides, there was widespread hostility to those who had allied themselves with the ravishers of Belgium and the killers of French, British and Irish soldiers. In fact, the rising was almost universally condemned. It seemed that the republican cause was lost. But this was far removed from what actually happened. It was Redmond and the Parliamentary Party which went into eclipse. The swing of nationalist opinion to the left was decided, in the main, by the mistake of the British Government in executing the rebel leaders, who were now looked on as martyrs in the cause of freedom. In these circumstances Redmond could get from the British Government no promise of an undivided Ireland; his programme had ceased to represent the wishes of the majority and his followers began to desert him.

THE 'TROUBLES'. Encouraged by the accumulating support for its aims, a Sinn Fein Convention in 1917 elected Mr De Valera President and requested him to arrange for Irish civil institutions to replace those controlled by the British. The people were to be exhorted to use these, and thus extend Griffith's principle of trade boycott to the spheres of law and civil administration. In the 1918 General Election the Sinn Fein Party – by now the political heirs to the separatist hopes of the leaders of the 1916 revolt – scored a tremendous success, winning 73 seats to the Unionists' 26 and Redmond's 6. In January 1919 Sinn Fein proclaimed the *Saorstat Eireann* or 'Irish Republic', thus ratifying the 1916 Proclamation.

These developments were viewed in England with considerable alarm. It seemed that if they went unchecked the security of the British Empire might well suffer. So repressive measures were taken. But these only served to strengthen the spirit of resistance. Lloyd George, the British Prime Minister, believing as he did in the principle of self-determination, was in a dilemma, for both the Sinn Fein and the Unionist leaders could claim its benefits. His solution of the difficulty was embodied in the Act of 1920, which gave each part of the country a parliament of its own for the handling of purely local affairs. Ulster accepted the scheme as the only possible alternative to saving the Union and in June 1921 King George V opened the Northern Ireland Parliament, with Sir James Craig as Prime Minister.

But it was a solution far from satisfying to the South, which considered that partition and self-determination were impossible bedfellows. The boycott of British institutions continued. Clashes between Sinn Fein sympathizers and the police were frequent. To assist the police in carrying out their difficult tasks, semi-military forces (the Black and Tans) and auxiliaries were recruited. Fierce guerrilla fighting soon broke out and spread throughout the country until in June 1921, Mr De Valera and Sir James Craig were invited to a conference in London to see what could be done to put an end to the bloodshed. Britain offered the Sinn Fein leaders an independence for Ireland similar to that of Canada or Australia, with full control over her own finances – a provision which, by its omission, had created a stumbling block in the 1912 Home Rule Bill. Though this did not satisfy De Valera, some of his colleagues persuaded him to consider it and in September he sent a delegation to London under Arthur Griffith with the object of trying to reconcile his own and their points of view. Griffith, without De Valera's authority, agreed to a scheme under which the only links between the two countries should be the King and Governor-General. Certain Irish ports were to be reserved as bases for the British Navy and Northern Ireland was to be allowed to decide for herself whether she should come under the Free State Government or not. These were the main provisions of the Irish Treaty.

De Valera, as expected, refused to accept these, and when they were debated and finally approved by the Irish Dail (by a majority of only seven votes) he resigned his post and Arthur Griffith was elected President. Northern Ireland, again as expected, contracted out and the frontier between the two portions of the country was finally decided in 1925. But this was not the end of trouble in the South, where a considerable section of the people followed De Valera in rejecting the Treaty. President Griffith died in August 1922, and Michael Collins his old friend and ally, and Commander in Chief of the Free State Army, was killed in an ambush by the dissidents. William Cosgrave succeeded Griffith as President. Gradually armed hostilities came to an end. The country was heartily sick of such strife. Mr De Valera's party, which at first had refused to have any association with the Free State Government, at last agreed to send representatives to the Dail. It increased in strength until, in 1932, it became the largest single party and De Valera became Prime Minister. It was his policy, in pursuit of the ideal of complete political separation from Britain, to whittle down the terms of the Treaty, to exclude the King's signature from Bills passed by the Dail, and to regain control of the Treaty ports. In 1937 a new constitution for the Irish Free State was introduced following a plebiscite, one of its provisions being to change the name of the state to 'Ireland', or in the Irish language 'Eire'. Finally in 1948, when Mr Costello was Prime Minister, Eire severed its tenuous link with the British Commonwealth and the twenty-six counties became an independent republic. The dream of the leaders of the 1916 revolt had at last come true.

I

BIG HOUSE AND MUD CABIN

W. R. Hutchison

Summary

THE DEFEAT of James II by William of Orange reinforces the power of the Protestant 'ascendancy' in Ireland. There is a strong 'No Popery' spirit in Britain and Ireland. In Ireland the Episcopalian minority is in control. The rights of Dissenters (mainly Presbyterian) are restricted by law. Presbyterian emigration to America swells. Penal laws are in force against Roman Catholics. By 1782 the Penal Code is largely repealed.

English laws restrict Irish commerce (e.g. there are embargoes on trade with the colonies and a flourishing Irish woollen trade is suppressed) yet the prosperity of the merchant classes increases, especially in the north. The landowning class are on the whole most affluent and prodigal. The linen industry is the mainstay of northern prosperity and Belfast increases its wealth and influence.

Protestant nationalism grows and is reflected in the Irish Parliament. When there is threat of invasion from France a national (exclusively Protestant) volunteer army is formed. In reaction to the injustices of church, state and landlords there is discontent among the poverty-stricken peasantry, leading ultimately to tension between Protestant and Catholic over acquisition of holdings.

TWO CENTURIES AGO Ireland was one country. But although it was one country with its own parliament in Dublin it was nevertheless divided in many ways. At the root of these divisions was religion. Most of the people were Roman Catholic and most of these Roman Catholics were the descendants of those who had inhabited the island for many centuries. They were the *native* Irish. Some Roman Catholics were the descendants of the Anglo-Normans and English who had come to Ireland in the Middle Ages.

The Protestants on the other hand were descended, for the most part, from those who in more recent days had come to conquer and garrison the country or who had been settled in it as colonists. With the Protestants lay the wealth and power of the country, a power which had been greatly increased by William of Orange's victories in the years 1690 and 1691. As a result, many leading Catholics had left their native land along with thousands of soldiers who had fought for the ill-fated James II.

Nevertheless, Roman Catholics were still in the majority, and Protestants felt insecure. And so the Irish Parliament, in defiance of the spirit of the treaty under which the Catholic armies had surrendered, passed a series of Anti-Catholic laws. This 'Penal Code', as it was called, degraded the majority of the Irish population.

Whereas it is notoriously known that the late rebellions in this kingdom have been contrived, promoted and carried on by Popish archbishops, bishops, Jesuits and other ecclesiastical persons of the Romish clergy. And forasmuch as the peace and publick safety of the kingdom is in danger, by the great number of the said archbishops which, not only endeavour to withdraw his majesty's subjects from their obedience, but do daily stir up and move sedition and rebellion. . .[1]

No Catholic may sit in the Irish parliament.

No Catholic may be a solicitor, game-keeper or constable.

No Catholic may possess a horse of greater value than £5. Any Protestant offering that sum can take possession of the hunter or carriage horse of his Roman Catholic neighbour.

No Catholic may attend a university, keep a school, or send his children to be educated abroad. £10 reward is offered for the discovery of a Roman Catholic schoolmaster.

No Catholic may live in Limerick or Galway or purchase property within their walls.

No Catholic may buy land or receive it as a gift from a Protestant.

No Catholic may be the guardian of a child. The orphan children of Catholics must be brought up as Protestants.

No Catholic shall on pain of death. . .

In fact as Chief Justice Robinson said:

The law does not suppose any such person to exist as an Irish Roman Catholic.[2]

But the barrier between Protestant and Catholic was not the only religious barrier in eighteenth-century Ireland. The Protestants themselves were divided into 'Church of Ireland' – the Established Church – and 'Dissenters' who were mainly Presbyterians. Although these Presbyterian Dissenters had fought with William of Orange against the Catholic armies of King James they were still in an under-privileged position. They were better off than the Catholics but were nevertheless denied many civil rights, particularly those which would have given them a share in the running of their country.

And so in the Parliament in Dublin sat only the representatives of the wealthy landowners of the Established Church. Little wonder that members of this church were called the 'Protestant Ascendancy'.

And yet they too had their grievances. The Irish Parliament was hamstrung by the British Parliament. It could only make laws of which the British Government approved and laws could be made in Britain by which the Irish were bound. Some of these laws were designed to restrict Irish trade so that English trade could flourish and these hurt Catholic and Protestant, Presbyterian merchant and Ascendancy landowner alike. Indeed it was a leader of the Ascendancy itself who wrote in a pamphlet:

I would be glad to know by what secret method it is that we grow a rich and flourishing people, without liberty, trade, manufactures, inhabitants, money or the Privilege of Coining; if we do flourish, it must be against every law of nature and reason, like the Thorn at Glastonbury that blossoms in the midst of winter.[3]

So wrote Jonathan Swift, Dean of St Patrick's Cathedral in Dublin, and author of the well-known book *Gulliver's Travels*. As a young man he had worked in the parish of Kilroot in County Antrim and had seen for himself how much trade restrictions like those on the export of wool were hurting industry.

Dr Vesey, Archbishop of Tuam, another member of the Established Church, wrote:

Ireland will never be happy until a law is made for burning everything that comes from England except her coals.[4]

And yet in spite of English laws the prosperity of the country was increasing. This increase was most marked in the north where the linen industry flourished. Belfast was growing in consequence and a prosperous Protestant merchant class was growing too.

Dublin was, of course, the capital city of Ireland and the centre of social as well as political and business life. In 1765 it had about 120,000 inhabitants. Cork at the same date had 60,000, Limerick 25,000 and Belfast a mere 8,000. But as the century wore on Belfast rapidly became the centre of a thriving industrial area and by the end of the century its population had trebled.

The prosperity of Belfast as compared with that of Dublin is reflected in a letter written by a Mrs McTier of Belfast. From her letters we learn much interesting information about the city in which she lived. She had no high opinion of its culture and elegance but she was certainly impressed by the way in which its inhabitants could spend money. She wrote:

You talk of a Dublin merchant paying one thousand guineas for furnishing a house. I heard a Belfast one's wife say she could not fit up her drawing-room for less.[5]

In Belfast we nor indeed anyone cannot live on a mere fortune except in an obscure and what is worse a vulgar manner. A small gentile house in a tolerable situation is not to be got at a moderate rent. The town is crowded with rich upstarts who skipping from the counter to their carriages run one down with the force of wealth which now gives them a lead in fashion, who a few years since would have shrunk with awe from the notion of what is called good company.[6]

And a friend of hers noted:

Though it is laid out in wide and straight streets which are carefully paved, clean, and well lighted, it has more attractions for the merchant than for the antiquarian.[7]

More attractions for the merchant! But not all the money of the newly rich, however, was spent on vulgar display. They were fond of the theatre and could appreciate good acting. Many famous performers were attracted to Belfast in the second half of the eighteenth century, and after a visit by the celebrated actress, Sarah Siddons, Mrs McTier confessed:

Her acting did credit to the feelings of the audience – Halliday swelled, Mattier snivelled, Major Leslie cried and damned the play. Waddell Cunningham rubbed his legs and changed his posture, Mrs Aderton was taken out in convulsions – hardly a man could stand it and many who withstood it in the house gave up to tears when they went home.[8]

But what of the other kind of moneyed class – the aristocratic landlords, the landed gentry, the agricultural Ascendancy. The eighteenth century saw the beginnings of scientific farming in England and, a few steps behind, in Ireland as well. Not only did crop rotation produce bigger and better harvests but animals too, because of turnip feeding, put on weight and sheep carried heavier fleeces. As a result tenant farmers could get more return for their labours and landlords were able to double or treble their rents.

The Irish eighteenth-century landlord – the gentleman of the big house – did not believe in hoarding or investing money. Instead he spent it on improving his house and his estate, on horses, on the upkeep of servants, on food, drink and on good living, all of which cost little in Ireland.

Lord Orrery described a dinner-party at which he was a guest:

Paper mills, thunder and the King's kitchen are soft music compared to the noises I have heard. Nonsense and wine have flowed in plenty, gigantic saddles of mutton and huge rumps of beef weighed down the table. Bumpers of claret and bowls of white wine were perpetually under my nose, till at last I slipt away leaving my hat and sword to be my representatives. I would have left an arm or a leg behind me rather than not have made an escape.[9]

And one Arthur Weldon wrote to his wife:

I believe my dearest wife will be surprised, and indeed angry, when I tell her that I went to bed last night at one of the clock, was on horseback this morning at four, rid eight miles before day-break, hunted a fox afterwards, came back here to dinner, and rid a coursing this afternoon until nightfall. I am inclined to be sleepy, so must bid you good-night with assuring you I am, my jewel, your own for ever ... A. Weldon.[10]

The celebrated English traveller Arthur Young wrote in 1780:

A landlord in Ireland can scarcely invent an order which a servant, labourer or cottar dares to refuse to execute. Nothing satisfies him but an unlimited submission. Disrespect or anything tending towards sauciness he may punish with his cane or his horsewhip with the most perfect security. It must strike the most careless traveller to see whole strings of cars whipt into a ditch by a gentleman's footman, to make way for his carriage; if they are overturned or broken to pieces, no matter, it is taken in patience; were they to complain they would perhaps be horsewhipped.[11]

Many of these landlords considered themselves to be great Irish patriots. They strove to increase Irish prosperity and above all they wanted to weaken the hold the English parliament had on their own parliament. When invasion threatened from France they went so far as to raise a national volunteer army equipped with splendid uniforms. Yet enough of them could be bought over by the Lord Lieutenant to maintain a majority willing to accept English control. And even the patriots of the Irish parliament had little sense of obligation towards the majority of the Irish people – the Roman Catholic peasants.

As the eighteenth century wore on the Penal Code had been largely repealed. Some Catholics were given the vote in 1793 but there was no thought of giving them outright political equality with Protestants. For example, they could not sit in parliament. Henry Flood, one of the leading figures amongst the Patriots in the Irish Parliament put it this way:

Ninety years ago four-fifths of Ireland were for King James. They were defeated. I rejoice in their defeat. The laws that followed were not laws of persecution, they were a political necessity. What will be the consequence if you give Catholics equal powers with Protestants? We will give all toleration to religion. We will not give them political power.[12]

And Henry Grattan, perhaps one of the most liberal Irish statesmen of his day and one who would have conceded much to the Roman Catholics, told the Protestant corporation of Dublin:

I love the Roman Catholic. I am a friend to his liberty, but it is only inasmuch as his liberty is entirely consistent with your ascendancy, and addition to the strength and freedom of the protestant community.[13]

What were the living conditions of the peasant like? Let it be said at the start that in the weaving country of the north they were much better than in the more purely agricultural south. But outside Ulster most peasants lived in squalid mud-walled cabins. They depended for food on potatoes and buttermilk. They had no money and no luxuries.

A traveller in Ireland towards the end of the century wrote of a night he spent in the home of a southern peasant.

Half a dozen children, almost naked, were sleeping on a little straw with a pig, a dog, a cat, two chickens and a duck. The poor woman spread a mat on a chest, the only piece of furniture in the house, and invited me to lie there. The animals saluted the first ray of the sun by their cries and began to look about for something to eat; the dog came to smell me; the pig put up her snout at me and began to grunt; the chickens and the duck began to eat my powder bag, and the children began to laugh. I got up very soon for fear of being devoured. I should add that I had no small difficulty in making my hostess accept a shilling.[14]

The majority of the population lived in conditions like these. Little wonder that towards the end of the century many peasants grew desperate.

In Ulster – the only province in Ireland where the Protestant religion spread through every social class – conditions may have been better but there was nevertheless widespread discontent. Many Presbyterians, whose forebears had come from Scotland to Ireland to carve out a new life free from religious intolerance, now thought they might find freedom again by emigrating to America. There they might have land of their own and perhaps an opportunity for riches.

By the end of the eighteenth century over a quarter of a million Ulster Presbyterians had crossed the Atlantic. But the majority of Irish peasants lived in squalor on a diet of potatoes and were not equipped to leave their native land. Many of them turned to armed violence. They formed secret organizations and did a good deal of damage to the property of landlords. At times they even committed murder.

But appalling living conditions were not the only cause of violence. There was sometimes bitter strife between Protestants and Roman Catholics, each side anxious to prevent the other from getting possession of land holdings. After one of these sectarian fights in County Armagh, Protestants had formed the Orange Order to protect their religion and their rights.

But the greatest threat to peace in Ireland had come from France where, in 1789, a revolution had overthrown the King and the ruling classes. In Ireland the Society of United Irishmen was formed in 1791. It was inspired by the ideals of the French revolutionaries and it began to sow seeds of discontent and rebellion throughout the country. The authorities very naturally became alarmed and took stern repressive measures. Suspects were arrested and brutally punished. A French traveller wrote of his experience in the neighbourhood of Banbridge:

Here I found soldiers going about the country burning the houses of suspected United Irishmen. Near to Armagh I met a group of Orangemen decorated with cockades. They were obliging everyone to take off every article of green they wore. I had a green string to my umbrella, and so, in fear lest I be mistaken for a rebel, I cut it off.[15]

It looked as though, sooner or later, discontent would flare up into open rebellion. Arms were stolen and stored away for future use. Secret messages went to and fro between Ireland and France.

The eighteenth century may have been a century of inequality, of rich property owner and humble peasant, of big house and mud cabin; nevertheless it had been a century of peace and progress. Now it seemed that the spade and the loom would be laid aside for the pike and the musket, that the big house would go up in flames.

> *At Boolavogue when the sun was setting,*
> *On the bright May meadows of Shelmalier,*
> *A rebel hand set the heather blazing,*
> *And brought the neighbours from far and near.*[16]

NOTES

1 Indexes to the Irish Statutes; a typical penal law of 1739. Quoted in Carty, J. *Ireland from the flight of the Earls to Grattan's parliament, 1607–1782*. Dublin: Fallon, 3rd edn 1957. p. 145.

2 Quoted by Lecky, W. E. H. *A history of Ireland in the eighteenth century* 5 vols. Longmans, 1892. vol. 1, p. 146.

3 From Swift, J. *Short view of the state of Ireland* Dublin, 1727. Quoted in Maxwell, C. *Dublin under the Georges, 1714–1830* Harrap, 1936. p. 25, or Faber, 3rd edn 1956. p. 32.

4 Froude, J. A. *The English in Ireland in the eighteenth century* 3 vols. Longmans, 1872–4. vol. 1, p. 502.

5 *The Drennan letters . . . 1776–1819*; ed. by D. A. Chart. Belfast: Northern Ireland, Public Record Office, 1931. p. 318. The letter is dated 3 June 1802, but has been used by Constantia Maxwell in *Country and town in Ireland under the Georges* Dundalk: Dundalgan P., 2nd edn 1949. p. 233, to create a picture of Belfast's prosperity in the late eighteenth century. Professor Maxwell prefaces the letter by saying 'at the end of the century [the eighteenth] the town [Belfast] had a prosperous air . . . and the merchants were as rich as, perhaps richer than, those of Cork and Dublin.'

6 Ibid.

7 Her friend was Sir Richard Colt Hoare. His observation is referred to in Maxwell, C. *Country and town in Ireland* op. cit. p. 244.

8 Young, R. M. *Historical notes on old Belfast and vicinity . . .* Belfast: Ward, 1896. p. 171.

9 Lord Orrery in a letter to Lord Waynright in 1737. Quoted in *Country and town in Ireland* op. cit. p. 25.

10 Written from Bishopscourt, 18 February 1726. Quoted in *Country and town in Ireland* op. cit. p. 33.

11 From Young, A. *A tour in Ireland . . . made in the years 1776, 1777 and 1778 . . . to the end of 1779* 2 vols. Dublin, 1780. Quoted in *A book of Ireland*; ed. by F. O'Connor. Collins, 1959. p. 264.

12 Froude. J. A. *The English in Ireland* op. cit. vol. 2, p. 306.

13 Quoted in Beckett, J. C. *A short history of Ireland* Hutchinson, 1952. p. 124.

14 From *A Frenchman's walk through Ireland, 1796–7* by Le Chevalier de La Tocnaye; trans. by J. Stevenson. Belfast and Dublin, 1917. Quoted in *A book of Ireland* op. cit. p. 128.

15 Le Chevalier de La Tocnaye, op. cit. Quoted in Maxwell, C. *The stranger in Ireland; from the reign of Elizabeth to the Great Famine* Cape, 1954. p. 204.

16 Composed by P. J. McCall, *circa* 1800. Published by Walton's Music, Dublin.

2

THE UNITED IRISHMEN

W. R. Hutchison

Summary

THEOBALD WOLFE TONE, carried away by the spirit of the French Revolution of 1789, founds the Society of United Irishmen in 1791. Though Protestant in origin it supports the political rights of Roman Catholics. The Protestant Ascendancy becomes alarmed, its alarm being intensified by the outbreak of war with France.

Repressive measures drive the United Irishmen underground and towards extremism and violence. They are strongest in the north where republican ideas, borrowed from America and France, have taken deepest root. Wartime economic depression stimulates agrarian unrest, which, in the north, becomes sectarian. In 1795, aggressively Protestant 'Orange' societies are founded.

With hope of French help, the United leaders determine on violent action. Meanwhile a well-briefed government vigorously crushes the revolutionary spirit and arrests several leaders. In 1798, the rebellion breaks out under local leadership.

French help having miscarried and with Tone himself in France, insurrection in Antrim and Down is quickly crushed. In Wexford, where religious grievances and resentment of military rule count for more than republicanism, the fighting lasts a little longer.

The rebellion, though itself a failure, has a profound effect on future nationalist movements.

> An Ulsterman I'm proud to be,
>   From Antrim's Glens I've come,
> And though I've laboured by the sea,
> I've followed fife and drum,
> I've heard the martial tramp of men,
> I've watched them fight and die,
> And well do I remember when,
> I followed Henry Joy.[1]

Last week you heard about some of the things that made Ireland a restless country in the last quarter of the eighteenth century. You heard about a minority of the population making a great deal of money out of linen and farming while the majority, the people who worked the looms and dug the fields, often found it difficult to earn enough money to pay for one square meal a day. Many of them were determined to force the authorities to attend to their grievances. And this they did by roaming the country at night, damaging the property of landlords and raiding houses for arms.

And you heard about other causes of unrest besides this; of the power of the Established Church, the Church of Ireland, and of the grievances of those who didn't belong to this church—especially the Roman Catholics. Indeed, Catholics and Dissenters, that is, Protestants who were not members of the Established Church, had nevertheless to contribute money to its upkeep.

Finally, you heard about a revolution which broke out in France in 1789. The power and privileges of the King of France and his nobles were overthrown, and all over the country castles went up in flames. A republic was set up. The King and his family and hundreds of nobles were executed at the guillotine. Under a republic, France would henceforth be ruled, not by a king, but by a parliament elected by the people and everybody was to have equal rights and privileges. This was following the example of America where French soldiers had helped the colonists to win their independence from Britain. In Ireland, many who wanted to change the way the country was governed were encouraged by the French Revolution. Others, though in favour of reform, were appalled and frightened by its violence.

But, the new French republic offered to help any small nation which was oppressed as they had been. Irishmen pricked up their ears. They began to hope that, with the help of the big French brother, they might at last see the end of their grievances. They did more than hope.

In 1791, Wolfe Tone, a Dublin lawyer and a Protestant, founded in Belfast, the Society of United Irishmen, whose object was to get rid of English influence once and for all and make the Irish as free and equal as the French were. He wrote a pamphlet about his aims:

Our provinces are ignorant of each other, uncemented like the image which Nebuchadnezzar saw, with a head of fine gold, legs of iron and feet of clay, parts that do not cleave together – we must unite them. That is

29

our end. The Rights of Man in Ireland, the greatest happiness of the greatest number in this island.[2]

But Wolfe Tone also knew that this new society of United Irishmen must move with caution:

Secrecy is necessary. It will make the spirit of union more ardent and more condensed. It will throw a veil over those individuals who might wish their activities to be concealed.[3]

But when Tone wrote his pamphlet, he did not say perhaps what he really felt, namely that satisfactory conditions for all could only be achieved in an Irish 'republic'. This might have frightened off moderate reformers. Yet when a candidate was being enrolled in the new society, in a lonely barn, maybe, in a tumble-down back room, or in a weaver's cottage, he was cross-examined as follows:

'Are you straight?'
'I am.'
'How straight?'
'As a rush.'
'What have you got in your hand?'
'A green bough.'
'Where did it first grow?'
'In America.'
'Where did it bud?'
'In France.'
'Where are you going to plant it?'
'In the crown of Great Britain.'[4]

So the numbers of the United Irishmen swelled and soon thousands of members were ready to obey Tone's orders and make Ireland a place of the greatest happiness of the greatest number. The leaders met and dined together and made plans for the future. Tone's diary describes one such meeting in the Grove Hotel, Belfast.

Breakfast with Simms. All the Catholics from Dublin there. Council of war in the garden. Simms says the thinking men are with us. Dinner, McTier in the chair. At the head of the table a Dissenter and a Catholic. Delightful. The four flags – America, France, Poland, Ireland, but no England. Bravo! Huzza! Three times three. God bless everybody.[5]

Meetings like this one in Belfast were held both in the north and south, but, in spite of efforts to keep them secret, there were informers who betrayed them to the Government.

This was a serious problem for the United leaders. Another problem was a growing split between Protestant and Roman Catholic members over the question of wanting a republic. The Catholics on the whole were much more concerned about land and landlords than in establishing an Irish republic. Indeed the leaders of their church considered French republicans to be dangerously irreligious. But it was to republican France that the Protestant members in Ulster looked for inspiration.

Republican ideas were discussed mainly in the homes of shopkeepers and weavers. Also in so-called 'reading societies'. As a writer to the *Belfast Newsletter* said:

In these societies labourers, tradesmen and even apprentice boys are taught to decide on matters of government and religion – to think themselves amply qualified to dethrone kings and regulate states and empires.[6]

But the activities of the United Irishmen were taking another form. Efforts were being made to seize arms. These were usually taken from private houses rather than from the military, which would have been too difficult. Innocent people were awakened up at midnight and ordered to hand over whatever weapons they had. If they refused, sometimes even if they had none to hand over, they were mercilessly beaten up. On more than one occasion there was outright murder.

All this resulted in the authorities taking reprisals no less ruthless. And there was violence of another sort also that had nothing to do with the United Irishmen movement. There was bitter competition for the possession of farms between Protestant and Catholic peasants especially in south Ulster. Rival groups often came to blows.

The most famous fight took place in 1795 at the Diamond, a village near Loughgall. Here at least thirty people were killed and after the battle the victorious Protestants met in the smoking ruins of a cottage and decided to form a new society. Their object was to defend their religion and hold their land against Catholic infiltration. Thus the Orange Order was founded, an event of great importance in the history of Ireland.

> Come all you loyal Orangemen and in full chorus join,
> Think on the deeds of William and his conquest at the Boyne,
> And gratefully commemorate that ever glorious day,
> That crowned the mighty hero King and ended Popish sway.[7]

Wolfe Tone was very distressed by all these divisions between Irishmen when they should have been combining their efforts against what he considered their real enemy – England.

He had gone to France to see if he could persuade the republican rulers of that country to send over an army as quickly as possible. He knew it wouldn't be an easy task. He was looked up to in Ireland as a forceful leader. To many he was a hero. But Ireland was a very small country. Thanks to Napoleon, France had become the most powerful country in Europe and had defeated the armies of Prussia, Spain and Austria. She was planning an attack on England. What kind of reception was Tone likely to have? As it happened his reception by Carnot the French War Minister, was better than he could have hoped. His diary tells about his first meeting:

Request to see Carnot. Clerk stares, but sends me up. Admitted. Carnot in white satin with crimson robe. In horrid French I said I was an Irishman, secretary and agent to three million Catholics in that country, and nine-hundred thousand Dissenters, all eager to throw off the yoke of England. He asked what we wanted. An armed force, I answered, with arms and a little money to begin with. He put many questions which showed he had been thinking the subject over. [8]

Tone was delighted. This, he thought, will put an end to divisions at home and get the rebellion started. He was given a commission in the French army and Carnot made preparations for an invasion fleet to sail to Ireland.

> O the French are on the sea,
>   Says the Shan Van Vocht,
> O the French are on the sea,
>   Says the Shan Van Vocht,
> O the French are on the say,
> They'll be here without delay,
> And the Orange will decay,
>   Says the Shan Van Vocht. [9]

On 15 December 1796 forty-three French ships with fifteen thousand picked troops on board, sailed from Brest. But alas for Tone's hopes, the expedition had bad luck from the start. The Commander, General Hoche, lost touch with the other ships in a fog and never turned up in Bantry Bay where they had arranged to meet. The second in command waited for a week, then when a bad storm blew up, gave the order to sail back to France. Tone, who was in one of the ships, wrote in his diary:

December 29th. At four this morning, the Commodore made the signal to steer to France; so there is an end of our expedition; perhaps for ever.[10]

So easy to land with only a handful of soldiers to oppose them! So easy to march on Dublin! It was not to be, and the United Irishmen began to lose heart. Should they not postpone the rising until more help arrived from France.

In the North the United leaders had made their decision; to rebel, French help or no French help. They had no real choice. The Government knew all their plans and had arrested some of their key men both in Belfast and at the Dublin headquarters. The most important of these was Lord Edward Fitzgerald who had played an important part in securing the interest of the French and to whom the United Irishmen were looking for information and leadership when the fighting would start. They must either rise at once – or wait to be picked up in batches.

In the early days of the United movement, Tone had met in Belfast a man of whom he thought highly. He was a cotton manufacturer and son of a sea captain. His name was Henry Joy McCracken. Though he lacked military experience, it was he to whom the County Antrim rebels now turned in their search for a leader. He accepted the responsibility, and in a very short time found himself in command of the rebel army, marching on the town of Antrim which was at that time a loyalist stronghold. He was a convinced republican, like most of his troops, and on the march they sang the new song of the French republic, 'The Marseillaise'.

> *Allons enfants de la patrie,*
> *Le jour de gloire est arrivé.*
> *Contre nous de la tyrannie*
> *L'étendard sanglant est levé,*
> *L'étendard sanglant est levé,*
> *Entendez vous dans les campagnes*
> *Mugir ces féroces soldats?*
> *Ils viennent, jusque dans nos bras,*
> *Egorger nos fils, nos compagnes!*
>
> > *Aux armes, citoyens!*
> > *Formez vos bataillons.*
> > *Marchez, marchez! qu'un sang impur*
> > *Abreuve nos sillons.*

It was all the help they had from France. The battle took place in the long, main street of the town. McCracken himself fought well and led his men well, but some of his officers disgraced themselves. In the words of an eye-witness:

One detachment had obeyed the Commander-in-Chief and forced the timid garrison. They were within a short distance of the appointed rendezvous when, meeting a corps of retreating cavalry, their leader mistook their flight for a charge and precipitately fled. This flight was more fatal than the most determined resistance would have been. Many were cut down with an unsparing hand and fell victims to that terror which too often plunges men into the very misfortune they seek to avoid.[11]

Though the rebels had a stronger force and better equipment than their enemies, they lost the battle. Any hope of success for the County Antrim men was now over. McCracken himself, after many adventures and narrow escapes at last found himself waiting in a peasant's hut a few miles from Belfast until arrangements could be made for him to board a ship that was due to sail from Larne to America. Half an hour before he was to be smuggled on board, however, he was betrayed to the military by a man whom he had known in his business days. He was arrested and kept in gaol to await his trial.

When this was taking place, an army officer tried to persuade both him and his father to save his life by betraying the name of the leader who had resigned and whose place he had taken. His sister, Mary Anne, describes the scene in her diary:

My father said, Mary my dear, I know nothing of the business, but you know best what you ought to do. Henry then said simply, Farewell father, and returned to the table to abide the issue of the trial. After I left him I was told that Major Fox went up to him and asked him for the last time if he would give any information, at which he smiled and said he wondered how Major Fox could suppose him such a villain.[12]

His refusal to talk meant that McCracken had to face death by hanging. He was executed beside the Old Market House where, in happier days, he had joined with a few friends in starting a Sunday School.

County Down did no better in the rising than County Antrim. At Ballynahinch, the United men under Henry Munroe were quickly crushed. In the south, after a series of victories in County Wexford, under Father Murphy and Bagenal Harvey, the United Irishmen were defeated at Vinegar Hill. There was still no sign of the long awaited French expedition. And then at last it came;

when the Irish fighting was over, when the rebels were thoroughly disheartened, when large numbers of those who escaped the hangman's rope had fled to America. And not only one expedition, but two.

The first arrived in Killala Bay, County Mayo, but was soon defeated. The second reached Lough Swilly, County Donegal. Wolfe Tone was on board the French flagship, but the squadron was intercepted by ships of the Royal Navy and the flag ship, abandoned to its fate by its supporters, had to fight a lone battle against impossible odds. It fought magnificently, but hopelessly. Tone was wearing his French uniform when he was captured. An historian has described what happened next.

The French officers were politely and hospitably received. They were invited to breakfast by Lord Cavan and Tone, who accompanied them, would have passed unnoticed at the table had he not himself rashly spoken to an acquaintance whom he encountered there. He professed to expect that his French Commission would protect him. He was painfully undeceived and ordered into irons as a traitor. He tore off his coat. These fetters, he said, shall never degrade the free nation which I have served. I feel prouder in my chains than if I was decorated with the Star and Garter of England.[13]

Later he was tried and sentenced to be hanged. But he died in prison; it is believed that he took his own life. So ended Wolfe Tone, founder of the United Irishmen. The man who had dreamed of an independent Irish Republic, who had had to cope with so many difficulties and disappointments.

By the end of the year 1798 the rebellion was over. William Pitt, the British Prime Minister, saw no way to solve the problem of Ireland but by joining it constitutionally to Britain. And so an Act of Union was passed in 1800, and Ireland lost her Parliament.

> It was for Ireland's cause we fought,
> For home and sire we bled,
> Our numbers were few but our hearts beat true,
> And five to one lay dead.
> And many's the lassie mourned her lad,
> And mother mourned her boy,
> For youth was strong in that gallant throng,
> That followed Henry Joy.

1 Anonymous. *Circa* 1800.

2 Quoted in Froude, J. A. *The English in Ireland in the eighteenth century* 3 vols. Longmans, 1881. vol. 3, pp. 12–13.

3 Ibid. p. 12.

4 Madden, R. R. *The United Irishmen, their lives and times* series I, vol. II, 1842. p. 37, appendix 12. A similar ritual is quoted in Pollard, H. B. C. *Secret societies in Ireland, their rise and progress,* Allan, 1922. p. 38.

5 From Tone's *Journal,* a much abridged version of his entry for 16 July 1792. Quoted in Tone, W. T. W. ed. *Life of Theobald Wolfe Tone*; written by himself . . . edited by his son. 2 vols. Washington: Gales and Seaton, 1826. vol. 1. p. 161.

6 Archives of *The Newsletter.* Date uncertain.

7 Anonymous. Nineteenth century.

8 Much abridged from Tone's entry for 24 February 1796. Quoted in *Life of Theobald Wolfe Tone* op. cit. vol. 2, pp. 25–26.

9 Anonymous.

10 Quoted in *A book of Ireland*; ed. by F. O'Connor. Collins, 1959. p. 107.

11 From *The personal narrative of the Irish Rebellion of 1798* by Charles Teeling. 1828. Quoted in Maxwell, W. H. *History of the Irish Rebellion in 1798* Baily, 1845, 4th edn 1854. p. 208.

12 Young, R. M. *Historical notes on old Belfast and vicinity* . . . Belfast: Ward, 1896. p. 186.

13 Froude, J. A. *The English in Ireland* op. cit. vol. 3, p. 542.

3

DANIEL O'CONNELL

Norman Harrison

Summary

THE ACT OF UNION is passed in an attempt to merge Great Britain and Ireland into one 'United Kingdom' with one parliament. The majority of Irish people do not benefit economically from union with the richer community. The privileged position of the Protestant Ascendancy is maintained. Most of Roman Catholic Ireland is in a state of wretched poverty.

Nationalism is revived by Daniel O'Connell and becomes closely associated with the interests of the Roman Catholic church. O'Connell condemns the Union, urges its repeal and wins popular support for 'catholic emancipation' – in particular the right of Roman Catholics to sit in Parliament.

O'Connell eschews violent revolutionary methods; relies on agitation and monster meetings. A Catholic Association is formed and funds are provided by the collection of 'catholic rent'. Though repeal of the Union is his principal aim O'Connell makes emancipation his first target. Resistance to emancipation crumbles after his own election as M.P. for Clare in 1828. Parliament is opened to Roman Catholics throughout the United Kingdom in 1829.

In Parliament O'Connell builds up a party of his own. He succeeds only partially in achieving reform in the system of 'tithes' under which the majority must subscribe to the upkeep of the Established Church (the church of the ascendancy minority). His repeal movement has little sympathy in England and meets strong opposition amongst Irish Protestants especially in Ulster.

In 1843 a monster meeting is banned by the Government; O'Connell cancels the meeting. His prestige consequently suffers while the influence of the Young Irelanders – a new nationalist group in the '98 tradition – is enhanced.

By 1845 the rift between the Young Irelanders and O'Connell is wide. O'Connell is no longer the popular leader. His health has broken, the potato famine has begun, and in its worst year, 1847, he dies.

I N THE LAST TWO broadcasts you heard about conditions in Ireland in the eighteenth century and of a people sharply divided in several ways. The root of Ireland's divisions was not hard to find. She was, after all, a country which, though the majority of her people were Roman Catholics of an ancient Irish race, was ruled by a Protestant Parliament under the influence of Britain.

You heard how in 1800 the Act of Union abolished the Irish Parliament. Henceforth Ireland was to be ruled by the Parliament at Westminster.

An Irish nation, left alone and seething as it was, might play host to one of Britain's enemies. Britain was now at war with

France – might not the Irish once again invite help from France as they had done in the '98 Rebellion? And so the Dublin Parliament was bribed to vote itself out of existence, and the Union was accomplished. To many Irishmen it seemed like a deathblow to their country, but Henry Grattan, under whose leadership the Parliament had brought increasing prosperity to Ireland, said this:

I do not give up my country. I see her in a swoon, but she is not dead; though in her tomb she lies helpless and motionless, still on her lips is the spirit of life.[1]

But who was to revive that spirit? In 1803 a young man called Robert Emmet tried. He led a revolt against the Union which failed because it had no widely organized support and Emmet was hanged. Yet the spirit was revived, for there emerged another young man, a new champion with new ideas who, for the first time in Irish history, offered to the majority of his country's people the leader they needed. His name was Daniel O'Connell.

> O'Connell is the man who adopted a new plan
> And is seeking for the rights of this nation
> His enemies will know that he can them overthrow
> And bring to us all emancipation.[2]

In the year the Act of Union was passed, Daniel O'Connell was a young Roman Catholic lawyer of twenty-six, but already he was taking a leading part in Catholic affairs. He knew very well the awful conditions in which his Catholic countrymen existed. But it was their lack of concern for their own hopeless position that moved him most.

O'Connell determined to rouse them, to show them how down-trodden they were – above all, to give them a cause for which they could unite and fight. That cause was Roman Catholic Emancipation – full equal rights for Catholics: in particular, the right of a Catholic to become a Member of Parliament. But how does a people start to throw-off oppression? Did O'Connell intend to follow the example of Wolfe Tone and Robert Emmet and lead his people once again to bloodshed? Not O'Connell, for all through his life he said:

No human revolution is worth the shedding of one single drop of human blood.[3]

What then? The answer, said O'Connell, was agitation. Talk

to the people, travel the country, make speeches, rouse them to demand their rights – waken them up!

Soon the fiery words of the man people came to call the Agitator were thrilling vast audiences all over Ireland. D'Alton, the Irish historian, wrote of him:

He had all the qualities that go to make a successful agitator. His frame was that of Hercules. He spoke Irish and English with equal fluency, and could therefore reach the masses of the people. It was on an Irish hillside, in the presence of an immense crowd, that he was at his best. His voice rang out as clearly as a bell, and as he spoke his audience laughed or wept, grew sad or gay, raised their heads high with pride when he told them they were the finest peasantry in the world, or muttered curses against the government when he recounted its evil deeds.[4]

And thus Daniel O'Connell, the Agitator, travelled the country urging his Roman Catholic countrymen to stand up for themselves.

The Catholic cause is on its majestic march; its progress is rapid and obvious. It is cheered in its advance and aided by all that is dignified and dispassionate. And its success is just as certain as the return of tomorrow's eve.[5]

Strangely enough, it was not the Catholic cause that had turned O'Connell the lawyer into O'Connell the Agitator. It was the passing of the Act of Union – the Union of Great Britain and Ireland.

The year of the Union I was travelling through the mountain district from Killarney to Kildare. My heart was heavy with the loss Ireland had sustained. My soul felt dreary as I traversed the bleak solitudes. It was the union that first stirred me up to come forward in politics. I was maddened when I heard the bells of St Patrick's ringing out a joyous peal for Ireland's degradation, as if it was a glorious national festival. My blood boiled, and I vowed on that morning that the foul national dishonour should not last, if ever I could put an end to it.[6]

But the chances of repealing the Union were slender. O'Connell was not only up against the Parliament in England, but against many people too, in his own country, who favoured the Union because they could profit by it – merchants who hoped to increase their business; and the so-called Protestant 'Ascendancy', the ruling class, whose power the Union maintained.

Yet O'Connell the Agitator would not see that his task was impossible. Hopeless as it was, he tried, as Wolfe Tone had tried, to bring all Irishmen together for this great purpose.

The Protestant alone could not expect to liberate his country – the Roman Catholic alone could not do it – neither could the Presbyterian, but amalgamate the three into the Irishmen, and the Union is defeated.[7]

But how could this be brought about? Religious differences seemed to be growing more bitter, and O'Connell was accusing the Government in London of creating these differences in order to weaken Irish unity. Had not the Duke of Wellington, a British Prime Minister, written:

The Protestants of Ireland may rely upon it that their existence and the possession of their properties depend upon the maintenance of the Union.

I have always considered O'Connell as the personification of the Roman Catholic religion in Ireland. The Roman Catholics as a body, rebels or pretended loyal subjects, follow him. I would earnestly recommend to the Protestants of Ireland to take a course entirely different. Let the question of Repeal or no Repeal be a question of Protestant and Catholic.[8]

It is little wonder, then, that O'Connell came to be looked upon as the spokesman for Roman Catholics rather than the mouthpiece of all the people of Ireland, and despite all his appeals, this was to haunt his work, especially in his dealings with Ulster.

In 1823 he formed a Catholic Association. There had been Catholic Associations before, but this one quickly got very wide support, including support from the Catholic clergy, and soon the Church was helping O'Connell to collect what he called a Catholic Rent of one penny per household per month. With this money the Association helped its people to fight cases in the law courts, to resist landlords, to tell the world of its work, in newspapers and pamphlets.

Soon the whole land was organized, and it looked as if, at last, as O'Connell had said, the Catholic cause was on its majestic march. The Duke of Wellington, for one, was worried.

If we cannot get rid of the Catholic Association we must look to Civil War in Ireland sooner or later.[9]

An Act of Parliament was passed in 1825, and by it the Association was suppressed. But O'Connell immediately started what he called the New Catholic Association and the work went on as before.

At an election in 1826, the Association helped to contest seats against members of powerful Protestant families. Then, in 1828, O'Connell himself was elected as M.P. for Clare. This was sensational, for it meant that many seats in Ireland might be wrested from the Protestant Ascendancy.

The man whom O'Connell had defeated, Fitzgerald, had, along with many other Protestants, been a supporter of Emancipation, yet on the day the result was declared he wrote at once to the Prime Minister.

Such a tremendous prospect as it opens up! For the degradation of the country I feel deeply, and the organisation exhibited is so complete and so formidable that no man can contemplate without alarm what is to follow in this wretched country.[10]

And the very next year, 1829, the Emancipation Act was passed at Westminster. Civil and religious rights for Roman Catholics throughout the United Kingdom had been won. Opinion in Britain on Catholic Emancipation had been almost equally divided. The Clare election had tipped the scale. From henceforth Daniel O'Connell would be known as *The Liberator*.

But in every country, much depends on the spirit in which laws are administered, and the administration of law in Ireland still remained in Protestant hands.

The landlord, in spite of the Emancipation Act, could still squeeze high rents and underpay his labourers, while the scanty earnings of the Catholic masses went as 'tithes' to maintain a church which they abhorred. One-tenth of each man's crop, no matter how miserable it was, had to be paid to the clergy of the Church of Ireland – not only by members of that church, but by Presbyterians and by Catholics too.

So O'Connell returned to the attack. He was a Member of Parliament now at Westminster, and it was not long before they felt his great power, right on their own doorstep. He was admired, but more often he was feared and hated.

In London *The Times* newspaper wrote of him:

> *Scum condensed of Irish bog!*
> *Ruffian, coward, demagogue,*
> *Boundless liar, base detractor,*
> *Nurse of murders, treasons factor*
> *Of Pope and priest the crouching slave*
> *While thy lips of treason rave.*
> *Ireland's peasants feed thy purse,*
> *Still thou art her bane and curse.*[11]

Certainly most of Ireland's peasants were ready to act together if O'Connell said so. And on the question of paying tithes to the Church of Ireland his instructions were direct and simple.

Refuse to pay. Refuse to pay.

Tithes could not be collected, and the Government had to yield again. In 1838 a Tithe Act was passed. It did not lift all the burden, but again it was victory.

Emancipation and tithes – but the most important objective still remained: Repeal. Repeal of the Act of Union which had deprived Ireland of her Parliament. In this cause he could count on little sympathy in Britain. But he would work again with the tools he had used before – agitation, monster meetings, speeches in the House of Commons. But would the Agitator, now sure of his power, be ready to use more than these?

He is no statesman who does not recollect the might that slumbers in a peasant's arms; and when you multiply that might by vulgar arithmetic to 600 or 700,000, is a man statesman or driveller who expects that might will always slumber amidst grievances continued or oppression endured too long?[12]

Seven hundred thousand Irishmen! But these did not include the Protestants of the North who now feared the strength of the Roman Catholics more than they had ever doubted the intentions of the British.

The scoundrel Orangemen, always enemies to Ireland, now place all their claims to England and government support. I have two objects – to overthrow the Orange system, and to convince the most sceptical that nothing but a domestic parliament will do Ireland justice.[13]

Perhaps he was a little optimistic when he travelled north to Belfast in 1843 to try to rally Ulster support.

A famous Presbyterian minister, Dr Henry Cooke, encouraged his flock to make things hot for O'Connell, and certainly the Orangemen did, for they broke the windows of his hotel in Belfast and of the hall where he was to speak. He never returned to Ulster.

> O'Connell he does boast of his great big rebel host,
> He says they are ten million in number,
> But half of them you'll find they are both lame and blind,
> For we're the Bright Orange Heroes of Comber.[14]

By this time he was sixty-eight, and outside Ulster he was still able to draw the crowds to his monster meetings. But the stormy tide of Repeal agitation had floated to the surface a group of young men who later became known as the Young Ireland Party. They did not waver as they thought O'Connell did. They would not be satisfied with good government instead of self-government. Their ways were different from his.

War – the exposure of ourselves to wounds, toil and death – is as much our duty in a just cause as any other mode of sustaining justice.[15]

We feel no wish to encourage the occasion of war, but whenever the occasion comes, may bold hearts and strong arms be found to plan, lead and fight.[16]

Eighteen forty-three, and O'Connell planned a great monster meeting at Clontarf, near Dublin, to take place on Sunday, 8 October. Would he now give his followers the signal to rise in rebellion – armed rebellion? But British troops had been pouring into Ireland. Sir Robert Peel, the Prime Minister, was studying O'Connell's every move and by now perhaps had the measure of him. He decided to call O'Connell's bluff; at the last minute the meeting was banned.

O'Connell had opposed the Government before. The meeting would go on. But when dawn came that Sunday, Clontarf was occupied by soldiers. The guns of the fort pointed at the meeting place, and out in Dublin Bay there was a line of warships. People had thought that O'Connell would stand firm. In fact he had already yielded and had cancelled the meeting himself. Sir Robert Peel had won the round.

It was clear now that the Government need not give way to O'Connell's methods any more, so it felt quite safe in punishing the leaders of the Repeal Movement. O'Connell was arrested and spent a year in prison. When he was released, he was still the hero, the agitator, the liberator; but his force was spent, and besides, the Young Ireland Party was attracting more and more of his supporters.

He made his last visit to Parliament in January 1847, to speak once again for his countrymen. Not Repeal this time – starvation, for a blight had struck the potato crop and Ireland was passing through one of the darkest hours in her history. But the old man's health was broken; his voice was thin and weak and his words could hardly be heard, and what he said went unheeded. His doctors sent him abroad. He set off for Rome, but all his strength had gone, and in Genoa on 15 May 1847, O'Connell, the Liberator died.

> *If he were but living, that here undaunted;*
> *He struggled through life to have liberty planted.*
> *But now his sad loss we do sorely lament it,*
> *Brave Daniel the chieftain of Erin go Bragh.*[17]

NOTES

1 In the Irish Parliament. Quoted in Curtis, E. *A history of Ireland* Methuen, 1936, 6th edn 1950; University paperback, 1961. p. 350.

2 Nineteenth century, anonymous.

3 Quoted in Gwynn, D. *Daniel O'Connell, the Irish liberator* Hutchinson, 1930. p. 239.

4 Quoted in D'Alton, E. A. *History of Ireland* 6 vols. Gresham, 1912. vol. 5, 1782–1879. p. 121.

5 Quoted in Gwynn, D. *Daniel O'Connell* op. cit. p. 102.

6 Daunt, W. H. O'Neill. *Personal recollections of the late Daniel O'Connell M.P.* 2 vols. Chapman, 1848. vol. 1. pp. 202–3.

7 O'Connell, D. *Life and speeches*, ed. by J. O'Connell. 2 vols. Dublin, 1846. vol. 1, p. 17 et seq.

8 From Wellington, Arthur Wellesley, 1st duke of. *Despatches* 8 vols. Murray, 1867–80, vol. 8, p. 497 et seq.

9 In a letter to Sir Robert Peel, quoted in MacDonagh, M. *Daniel O'Connell and the story of catholic emancipation* Dublin and Cork: Talbot P., 1929. p. 134.

10 In a letter to Sir Robert Peel, 5 July 1828.

11 Quoted in Gwynn, D. *Daniel O'Connell* op. cit. p. 8.

12 At the banquet following the meeting at Tara Hill on 15 August 1843. Recorded in *The Nation* 19 August 1843.

13 In a letter to P. P. V. Fitzpatrick, 21 April 1835.

14 Anonymous. *Circa* 1843.

15 From *The Nation* 10 June 1843.

16 Ibid.

17 Anonymous.

4

THE FAMINE

Norman Harrison

Summary

IN THE EARLY nineteenth century the Irish peasant lives almost entirely on potatoes he grows himself. When the crop fails he has no money to buy anything else. His rent to the landlord is his labour, or his other crops (e.g. oats).

Partial failure of the potato crop in Autumn 1845 causes distress throughout Ireland. The Government is uncertain about the extent of the problem and about the appropriate action to take but imports Indian corn (maize) from America as a precaution.

The crop sown in 1846 is less because seed potatoes have been eaten for food. The crop again fails. The famine is at its height in the winter of 1846–7. Fever is rampant.

To alleviate distress the Government sanctions public works and attempts to distribute Indian meal. Bad administration and planning, corruption, misunderstanding of the true nature of the distress, and the fear of endangering the English economy, offset every good intention. Private charity is organized on an impressive scale at home and abroad; many landlords do their best for their tenants – often at great cost to themselves – but others behave callously. Evictions in some cases are enforced by constabulary and soldiers.

There is large-scale emigration, especially to Canada and the United States; many emigrants die on the way. Irish immigrants, rife with disease, and willing to work for lower wages, are on the whole unwelcome in the New World.

IN LAST WEEK's programme you heard how Daniel O'Connell roused and united the Roman Catholic peasants of Ireland to protest against union with England, against the tithe laws and against injustices that kept them almost in slavery. Some of that struggle they won.

Now we come to the story of a battle against nature, where the penalty of failure was death. Today's programme is the story of what happened in Ireland in the three years 1845, 1846 and 1847, three years that were the blackest in all her history.

> Oh the praties they are small over here, over here,
> Oh the praties they are small over here.
> Oh the praties they are small, and we dig them in the fall,
> And we eat them skins and all over here, over here.[1]

To the Irish peasant the potato was life. If the crop was a big one, he and his family had plenty to eat. If it was small, they went hungry. A peasant would rent a piece of ground from the landlord and on this land he would be allowed to build a cabin. He paid his rent by labouring for the landlord or else by bartering or selling his crops. In his day-to-day life he rarely, if ever, handled money. He had no luxuries, no means of buying food if his potato crop failed. And if his store of potatoes finished before his next crop was ready for harvesting, he faced starvation. No wonder the Duke of Wellington wrote:

I confess that the annually recurring starvation in Ireland gives me more uneasiness than any other evil existing in the United Kingdom.[2]

Ireland was used to hunger. Nobody worried much more than usual, therefore, when in 1845 a dramatic announcement appeared in an English journal:

We stop the press with very great regret to announce that the potato murrain has unequivocally declared itself in Ireland. The crops about Dublin are suddenly perishing.[3]

In fact, not only were the crops about Dublin perishing – in Antrim the failure was complete. Around Armagh there was hardly a sound potato. From Bantry and Donegal, from Tyrone and Wicklow came the same news – the potatoes were rotting, putrid in the fields. As the weeks went by, the outlook grew blacker and blacker. One of the most important landowners in Ireland warned the Prime Minister:

I do not recollect any former example of a calamitous failure being anything near so great and alarming as the present. I know not how the peasantry will get through the winter.[4]

And the medical officer of the Coleraine workhouse saw that more than hunger was to come.

46

Nothing else is heard of, nothing else is spoken of. Famine must be looked forward to and there will follow, as a natural consequence, typhus fever.[5]

The Government could be in no doubt now that calamity like a black cloud was lowering over Ireland.

The first action of Sir Robert Peel, the Prime Minister, was to appoint three professors to see if science could do anything to save at least some of the crop. The professors devised a scheme by which the labourer was to put his rotting mess of putrid potatoes through a long process and then mix the result with meal, oatmeal or flour. The men of science did not know that the Irish peasant had possibly never tasted oatmeal or flour.

The professors also printed 70,000 copies of these fantastic instructions for distribution to men who could not read. Meanwhile, the labourers were growing hungrier.

> *Oh I wish that we were geese, night and morn, night and morn,*
> *Oh I wish that we were geese, night and morn.*
> *Oh I wish that we were geese, then we all could be at peace,*
> *Till the time of our release, eating corn, eating corn.*

Hunger marched through the fields. Winter came. The cabbage leaves, the berries, the almost uneatable things that scavenging animals would usually hope for, were all gone, devoured by the starving people.

As a precautionary measure Peel had ordered £100,000 worth of Indian corn in the autumn – we know it as maize – to be bought in America and shipped to Ireland; but not to be given out free to the starving. This corn was to be sold in areas where for hundreds of square miles there were no shops nor indeed any system of distribution, and sold to people who not only had no money, but had no chance to earn it.

And all the time the oats and the wheat that they themselves had worked to grow were being shipped to England. Indian corn locked in depots and guarded by troops; the harvests of Ireland escorted by police or soldiers from the fields to the ships. This was more than famished people could stand. Yet worse was to come.

In 1846 the crop sown was less, for many of the potatoes set aside for seed had had to be used for food. But in any case it did not matter, for the crop failed again – totally this time. No part of Ireland escaped. Autumn 1846 walked hand in hand with death to meet the winter and 1847.

John Mitchel, a great Irish patriot, described his coming to a village in the west:

Why do we not see the smoke curling from these lowly chimneys? Surely we ought by this time to scent the turf fires. But what (may Heaven be about us this night) what reeking breath of hell is this oppressing the air?

There is a horrible silence; grass grows before the doors; we fear to look into any door, though they are all open or off the hinges, for we fear to see yellow chapless skeletons grinning there. We walk amidst the houses of the dead, and there is not one where we dare to enter. We stop before the threshold of our host of two years ago, put our head, with eyes shut, inside the door jamb and say with shaking voice *God save all here*. No answer. Ghastly silence and a mouldy stench as from the mouth of burial vaults. Ah! They are all dead; they are all dead![6]

But John Mitchel saw some of the living too.

Cowering wretches almost naked in the savage weather, prowling in turnip fields and endeavouring to grub up roots that had been left; groups and families sitting or wandering on the high road with failing steps and dim patient eyes.

And sometimes I could see in front of the cottages little children leaning against a fence – for they could not stand – their limbs fleshless, their bodies half naked, their faces bloated yet wrinkled and of a pale greenish hue – children who could never, oh it was too plain, grow up to be men and women.[7]

No Government could ignore a part of its kingdom reduced to such desperate need, but the help that it gave seemed to be given almost with reluctance and hobbled by regulations and rules and conditions that showed appalling ignorance of the situation and of Ireland.

To bring employment, for instance, the Government sanctioned public works which usually means the making of roads or harbours or bridges for the public good. Yet a paper called *The Nation* wrote:

There was a distinct order issued that works were not to be commenced without the existence of distress and not to be carried beyond that point. And so it was judged safest to set people to some sham work, like cutting down a hill. Perhaps a road was started where a road was needed; the order would arrive that distress in that area was over and all the work would stop, and the labourers sent about their business, and all their labour would be utterly thrown away.[8]

Bad planning, bad handling, confusion and often cheating and corruption seemed to follow Government attempts at relieving distress. Depots full of maize were still guarded by police, but the food could be bought, if you had money enough.

Mothers worn down to skeletons, sad and heartbroken, were seen on certain days proceeding to some depot where Indian meal was to be had at a reduced price – but still double that of the ordinary market.[9]

Still double that of the ordinary market, because of an order issued by Sir Randolph Routh, the man in charge of relief in Ireland.

In no circumstances are traders to be undersold and therefore no prices are to be fixed which would not enable traders selling at the same price to realise their profits.[10]

Then there came a time when the depots, though still guarded by police, were empty, because the Government had stopped buying food to prevent prices in England from rising. As Sir Randolph put it:

And you cannot transfer famine from one country to another. You cannot expect the English and Scottish labourers to support Ireland and pay famine prices as well.[11]

So the Irish could starve, as long as the balance of trade was not upset. And starve they did.

To meet the mother returning home empty from the depot – that was misery indeed. She had no money, could obtain no credit. Yesterday, no breakfast, no dinner, no supper – the same today – no prospect of better tomorrow. Overpowered by hunger, thousands, aye, hundreds of thousands have sunk down, sickened and died.[12]

Sir Robert Peel gave Parliament another reason why the Government was not doing more.

While Parliament is sitting there can be no difficulty in obtaining such further measures as may be needed, but I think the honourable and learned gentleman will agree with me that it is wise not to be too liberal. The great dependence must of course be upon the spontaneous charity of the landed proprietors and others. There is an undoubted claim upon the landowners who will not fail to come forward at this period of general distress.[13]

But the landowners as a body did fail to come forward. Many of them helped, and *The Nation* could publish lists of landlords who were reducing or cancelling rents. Nevertheless hundreds of tenants in small cottages and cabins were evicted for non-payment of rent with a callousness impossible to understand: the house was often pulled down, the people cast out no matter the weather. In a village in County Galway forty-seven people were thrown bodily out of their homes by a force of policemen. All over Ireland starving men, women and children were cast into the fields, and they passed on hopelessly to join the thousands of half skeletons wandering the roads.

No wonder that desperate things were done, such as you hear of in the famine songs written at the time:

> It was early one morning just before the break of day,
> The landlord and the sheriff came by without delay.
> They broke the doors and windows, it was an awful sight,
> To see my aged parents by the hedge that frosty night.
>
> The landlord spoke most roughly, which caused his sad downfall,
> For through his perjured body, I drove a pistol ball,
> In running fast to get away I chanced to look behind
> And saw a mounted policeman and he riding like the wind.[14]

But violence was not the answer, and in any case the country was teeming with troops. Famished and penniless people could do nothing except wish, as one of them did in Ballinrobe as the Seventh Hussars came into the town.

Would to God the Government would send us food instead of soldiers.[15]

But if the Government was not sending enough, other people were trying. Irishmen in the Indian army sent £50,000. A private committee in Dublin collected £63,000. The Society of Friends – the Quakers – helped in many ways and the generosity and humanity of the English public brought this tribute from O'Connell.

If the exhibition of those qualities by individuals could save Ireland in her present misery, we should be saved.[16]

Perhaps America was most generous of all. But it was never enough – private charity, Indian corn, public works. They only postponed the answer. And John Mitchel could write:

We knew the whole story – the father was on a *public work* and earned the sixth part of what could have maintained his family, which was not always duly paid him; but still, it kept them half alive for three months, and so instead of dying in December, they died in March.[17]

Horror piled on horror. While the lucky ones died by the side of the road, the others shambled where rumour led – rumour that said it was now easier to get into a workhouse, and by a change in the law it was easier.

So they flocked to the towns, weak and dirty; and, packed together, warm for the first time in months, they made an excellent hothouse for typhus fever. Death struck again, savagely. Ireland was gripped by a fever epidemic that slashed like a scythe in a field. Nobody knows how many people died – in Belfast alone 17,000 cases were treated, and deaths from fever in Ulster, which suffered least, were 33,000. Over the country to join the shadow of hunger and the cloud of disease came the pall of hopelessness.

A calm still horror was over all the land. Go where you would, in the heart of the town or in the church, there was the stillness and feeling of the chamber of death.[18]

Emigration became an industry. It was death to stay in Ireland, so the drift of the hungry wandering ones turned towards the ports. It is reckoned that over one and a half million people crossed the Atlantic at this time. To the desperate victims of the 1840s, emigration meant hope. How could they know, boarding a ship in Belfast or Cork or Newry or Dublin to escape the pestilence and the hunger, that an immigration officer in the United States would later write:

If crosses and tombs could be erected on the water, the whole route of the emigrant vessels from Europe to America would long since have assumed the appearance of a crowded cemetery.[19]

It seemed as if there was a curse on these doomed people. Emigration was profitable and easy profits attracted speculators, and speculators sent people to sea in ships that sometimes were hardly out of sight of land before they sank. Coffin ships, history called them. And they carried a passenger who paid no fare – the fever! Survivors of the hunger on land now found death by fever on the green Atlantic. But thousands did reach America where many of them found that hope was still a far-off thing.

An inscription on a monument in Grosse Isle – one of the immigrant landing-places – tells a grim story:

In this secluded spot lie the mortal remains of 5,294 persons who, flying from pestilence and famine in Ireland in the year 1847, found in America but a grave.[20]

Those who did not die found a cold welcome in the new land. They were so desperate that they would work for almost nothing and thus they brought down other people's wages. Any dwelling-place must be better than the hovels they had left in Ireland, and so they were content to live in slums. It was like this in any of the countries to which the famine drove them – America, Canada, England or Scotland. And in all these lands the Irish still remember the famine.

> *O we're down into the dust, over here, over here,*
> *O we're down into the dust, over here.*
> *O we're down into the dust, but the Lord in whom we trust*
> *Will return us crumb for crust, over here, over here.*

NOTES

1 *The famine song*, anonymous. Opinion is divided as to whether this song is Irish or American in origin.

2 From Wellington, Arthur Wellesley, 1st duke of. *Despatches* 8 vols. Murray, 1867–80. vol. 3, pp. 111–112. Wellington to Northumberland, 7 July 1830.

3 Dr Lindley writing in the *Gardeners' Chronicle*, 13 September 1845.

4 Quoted in Woodham-Smith, C. *The great hunger, Ireland 1845–9* H. Hamilton, 1962. p. 48.

5 Ibid.

6 John Mitchel writing in *The Nation* 19 June 1847.

7 Mitchel, J. *The last conquest of Ireland (perhaps)* Dublin and Glasgow, 1861. pp. 207–208.

8 *The Nation* 29 August 1846. The reference was to a report of a Select Committee of the House of Commons. The admission was made by the Chancellor of the Exchequer.

9 Quoted in Carty, J. *A classbook of Irish history* book IV, Dublin: St Martin's, 1959. p. 43. The description is of conditions in Wicklow in the winter of 1846–7.

10 Routh in a circular to a relief committee in the west, 18 October 1846. Quoted in Woodham-Smith, C. *The great hunger* op. cit. pp. 132–133.

11 Charles Edward Trevelyan, Assistant Secretary to the Treasury in a letter written to Colonel Harry Jones, Chairman of the Board of Works, Ireland, 5 October 1846.

12 Carty, J. *Classbook* book IV, op. cit. p. 43. Wicklow.

13 Sir Robert Peel in a reply to Daniel O'Connell in the House of Commons. Quoted in *The Nation* 14 March 1846.

14 *The landlord eviction* Anonymous, *circa* 1850.

15 Quoted in Woodham-Smith, C. *The great hunger* op. cit. p. 137.

16 In a letter to a friend.

17 John Mitchel in *The Nation* 19 June 1847.

18 John Mitchel. Quoted in *A book of Ireland*; ed. by F. O'Connor. Collins, 1959. p. 113.

19 Woodham-Smith, C. *The great hunger* op. cit. p. 238.

20 Ibid. p. 237.

5

INDUSTRIAL REVOLUTION

David Hammond

Summary

THE INDUSTRIAL REVOLUTION in Ireland brings a new way of life to many people throughout the country. Its effect is greatest in the province of Ulster.

After the Williamite war further restrictions are placed on Irish trade. To offset the crippling laws against the woollen trade (which threatens the English woollen trade) the manufacturing of linen is encouraged. Huguenot refugees are directed to the Lagan Valley early in the eighteenth century to develop modern techniques in spinning, weaving and bleaching. The linen industry spreads throughout Ulster as a 'cottage' industry closely associated with farming. Market towns grow in importance and linen exports increase throughout the eighteenth century.

In 1870 the cotton industry arrives in Ulster and is organized in a very different way from linen; raw material is imported and the yarn is spun by machinery in factories. Because fuel for motive power has to be imported, the industry in the north is confined mainly to Belfast. Belfast grows. Competition from cotton hits the linen weaver working in the countryside. Engineering industries associated with cotton machinery spring up in Belfast.

The cotton boom ends around 1830 in the face of competition from Lancashire. The industrial organization of cotton is now re-orientated towards the manufacture of linen. New machines and techniques are developed for linen manufacturing. Linen mills are built in the provincial towns. During the American Civil War the linen industry booms. Linen manufacturing in factory conditions is most injurious to the health of the workers.

In the 1840s a railway network is being developed. Belfast harbour is improved to cope with increased trade. The engineering activity, first stimulated by the cotton industry, now finds expression in shipbuilding. Under Messrs Harland and Wolff the shipyards expand in the nineteenth century.

The Industrial Revolution accentuates the differences between the north-east of Ireland and the rest of the country. Ulster is linked more closely with industrial Britain. Elsewhere in Ireland there is poverty, discontent and resentment towards the Union.

L AST WEEK YOU heard the story of the famine in Ireland, the horror that spread through the land, the nightmare of disease, hunger and death. Ireland was never the same again.

Today we are going to examine another important influence in our history, a process which was to change the face of Ulster, and give to many people a completely new way of life. This process of change extended over a period of years and was to become known as the Industrial Revolution.

Until after the Battle of the Boyne, Ulster was not in any way industrialized. There were few towns and these were small, existing as markets for butter, beef and wool. Carrickfergus was the nearest thing we had to a city and its population was barely 3,000 people; Belfast was only a small town though important as a port and a trading centre. We read in an old document:

In 1699 the linen trade was of no manner of consequence . . . the people were entirely ignorant of the art of managing and working flax, spinning yarn and whitening the cloth . . . they were absolute strangers to the looms.[1]

What made things worse was that the small Irish woollen trade was destroyed by laws passed to please English woollen manufacturers who saw Irish wool as a threat to their own woollen trade. Nevertheless, King William III felt that he owed some reward to the people of Ulster who had helped to give him the throne, so he promised to encourage the Irish linen trade. Linen would provide no threat to the prosperity of any Englishman. Accordingly a group of about 500 families of French protestant-refugees, Huguenots, were directed to Ireland. They settled in the district around Lisburn; they used their knowledge and skills to establish the most modern techniques of spinning, weaving and bleaching in the Lagan Valley. This settlement was decisive in concentrating linen-making in the north.

The linen trade spread throughout Ulster in the eighteenth century but was always closely associated with farming. The weavers were farmers who took on the extra occupation to eke out the living they wrought from their small plots of ground. They grew their own flax and the women-folk spun it into yarn, or else they got the yarn from the bleachers; and when the farmers had time from their work in the fields they wove the yarn into cloth on the hand-looms in their own homes.

> My wife the house trims up full-tidy
> And in her wheel sits down beside me
> All through the night my shuttle plays
> Tae keep my bairns warm in claes. . .[2]

While some cloth was kept at home to provide for their own families the bulk was intended for sale to the linen merchants at the fairs or back to the bleachers if they had supplied the yarn. The linen trade was essential to the Ulster farmer's livelihood though often, as the records tell us, it brought little reward when the weaver-farmer haggled for price with the linen merchant.

> My wee bit o labour bein thrown on the counter,
> Wi butterfly's een tae examine't he goes;
> He hemmed and he ha'd, and he swore it was shameless,
> Syne oot wi his snoot-cloot and dighted his nose.
> He swore that the warp would been better by double –
> For their penny collars twas nae use ava;
> Though the price o my labour was just half a guinea,
> He would gie me a shilling and let me awa. . .[3]

But a considerable quantity of cloth changed hands at the linen fairs that grew up in market towns like Lisburn, Dungannon, Dromore, Ballymoney and Bangor. It grew to represent a valuable export that increased steadily throughout the eighteenth century, as you can judge from these trading figures.

The year 1700: 170,000 yards of linen exported from Ireland.
The year 1800: 35,000,000 yards of linen exported from Ireland.[4]

TO20536

Now although these are the export figures for the whole country it is true to say that by the end of the eighteenth century the bulk of the linen was made in Ulster.

Linen-making was still an old-fashioned business carried on as a spare-time occupation in the homes of small farmers. Indeed, the only process to develop in the technical sense was bleaching which tended to be handed over to specialized firms as the quantity of linen increased during the eighteenth century. Here again the Lagan Valley, the cradle of the linen trade, with its ideal situation for collecting cloth from all over the province and the abundance of water for use in the bleaching process, was the centre of the industry. In addition there was the port of Belfast, now grown in importance, convenient for exporting direct to England. Belfast was growing as a linen market as well as a port. In 1739, a new Linen Hall was proposed.

. . . That as this north part of the Kingdom exceeds all other parts for making linens . . . of such height and perfection . . . and this port being a very safe one . . . and since shipping is very plenty to carry linen cloth to all parts of England it is not doubted that the erecting of a Linen Hall in this place will induce merchants who formerly bought in Dublin to buy here. . .[5]

Belfast got its Linen Hall and became a principal market for linen cloth and yarn, its trade increasing throughout the eighteenth century.

But a new industry arrived in Ulster in 1780, the industry that had heralded the industrial revolution in England, and an industry that was destined ultimately to swell the small town of Belfast into a city. It was cotton.

Now the cotton industry was organized in a way very different from linen – the raw material was foreign and it was spun by machinery. A man needed considerable capital to manufacture cotton – money to buy the raw material from overseas, money to set up his expensive machinery in mills and pay wages to employees. For the first time industry was taking people from their own homes and setting them to work in factories. And the very fact that raw material and fuel as well had to be imported restricted the spinning mills to Belfast.

Belfast started to expand. The Industrial Revolution had come to Belfast, if not to Ireland as a whole.

In 1811 an observer wrote about cotton:

Since 1800 the number of steam engines erected in a circuit 10 miles around Belfast is fifteen . . . driving 99,000 spindles; besides these there are six factories, the machinery wrought by horses, and twelve spinning mills driven by water containing 50,000 spindles . . . these all employ near 22,000 persons.[6]

The same writer also pointed out that there were about 40,000 persons working in the different branches of the cotton business in Ulster. But the linen weavers throughout the province saw in cotton and in the introduction of power looms for linen their ruination. They were, as you remember, poor farmers with no capital to invest in new machinery. They were the first victims of the new engines.

> An when I was rade an hale an young,
> My thread cam level, an fine as a hair,
> And the kitten purrd, and the cricket sung,
> And the care of my heart was a lightsome care
> Now men hae erected a new engine,
> An left out little for us to earn,
> An little for me but to pinch an pine
> I wish I had died when I was a bairn.[7]

And an observer wrote from Armagh in 1847:

. . . The weaver at home can earn only 2/6 to 4/6 . . . in a whole week . . . it will not support a mere weaver without a family. Weavers are sitting up three nights a week, in order to procure food for their families. . . I have seen them at 2.00 a.m. working as busily as in the daytime . . . often compelled by exhaustion to lie down. . .[8]

When linen-weavers found themselves unable to exist in the face of competition from lower-priced cotton, thousands of them throughout Ulster deserted their country homes and crowded into the cotton-spinning mills around Belfast, swelling its population. Others turned to cotton-weaving in their own homes.

But the days of the cotton boom in Belfast were short-lived for Ireland was not able to compete against the giant cotton industry in Lancashire. Still, even though cotton failed and disappeared almost entirely by 1830 it would be difficult to exaggerate its importance. For it was cotton that brought country people flocking into Belfast and it was the demand for cotton machinery that initiated the engineering industries of Belfast. And above all the industrial organization of cotton was the model for the reorganization of linen from home to factory.

Just as the cotton industry in Belfast was failing linen had its own revolution – a machine for wet-spinning flax was invented and it came into use in the mid-1820s.

By 1838 there were fifteen flax-spinning mills in Belfast and over the province bleaching firms were building flax-spinning mills at Lisburn, Bessbrook and Castlewellan. In places like Sion Mills and Dungannon where linen had been in deep depression the smoke stacks of huge mills were seen for the first time and workers left the countryside to settle in the growing towns. But many weavers remained at work in their homes to weave yarn spun in the new mills.

David Lindsay, a Dromore mill owner, hands out mill-spun flax yarn to 950 weavers in his district.[9]

But the Industrial Revolution in linen was concentrated almost entirely in the eastern half of Ulster.

In 1850 the counties of Down and Antrim accounted for three-quarters of the spinning of the whole country.[10]

By the middle of the nineteenth century Belfast was a town of over 100,000 people. When the American Civil War caused cotton to decline further even in Lancashire, linen boomed in Belfast and Belfast's chief industry rocketed in importance, but not without cost to human beings. Overcrowding in Belfast became a serious problem in the red-brick streets that mushroomed in the shadow of the mill stacks. Mutilation and death in the mills were frequent. The *Belfast News-letter* reported in May 1854.

On Saturday, a woman, Sarah Jane Quin, a worker in the mill . . . at York Street sustained a very severe accident . . . She was engaged at the carding part of the machinery and her head became entangled in the machinery, in which the greater part of her scalp was removed from the head and the skull severely injured. Little hope was entertained of her recovery.[11]

Sarah Jane Quin was only one of many. Perhaps the most terrible aspect of conditions in the linen industry were the hardships suffered by women and children. Poverty was so widespread that the combined efforts of the entire family, father, mother and children were demanded.

> *O dear me the mill's going fast,*
> *Poor wee doffers cannot get their rest,*
> *Shifting bobbins coarse and fine –*
> *They fairly make you work for your ten and nine.*

Henry Grattan addressing the Irish Parliament
Belfast 1792. Volunteers commemorate the destruction of the Bastille

Theobald Wolfe Tone 1763–98
The Battle of Antrim 1798

Daniel O'Connell 1775–1847
O'Connell as seen by an English cartoonist

KING O'CONNELL AT TARA.

The potato famine 1845–47. A destitute family
Roll call on an emigrant ship

Manchester 1867. Fenians attack a prison van

1881. Mr Parnell is escorted from the House for obstructing parliamentary business

County Clare 1888. Eviction of tenants by police and military
William Ewart Gladstone introducing the Home Rule Bill of 1886

A unionist cartoon of 1912

*John Redmond led the Irish Party
at Westminster 1900–18*

The Irish Citizen Army, formed in 1913 after the Dublin transport strike

Sir Edward Carson, leader of the anti-Home Rule protest

Belfast 1914. Carson inspects the Ulster Volunteer Force
1914. The Asgard at Howth with rifles for the Irish Volunteers

Mr de Valera taking part in the gun-running at Howth
The Easter rising 1916. The aftermath

Michael Collins and Eamon de Valera 1921

Black and Tans. The markings indicate men wanted by the Volunteers

months from the date hereof.

18. This instrument shall be submitted forthwith by His Majesty's Government for the approval of Parliament, and by the Irish signatories to a meeting summoned for the purpose of the members elected to sit in the House of Commons of Southern Ireland, and if approved shall be ratified by the necessary legislation.

Decr 6th 1921.

On behalf of the British Delegation

D Lloyd George

Austen Chamberlain

Birkenhead.

Winston S. Churchill

L. Worthington Evans

Hamar Greenwood

Gordon Hewart.

On behalf of the Irish Delegation

Ard ó Griobhta (Arthur Griffith)

Mícheál ó Coileáin

Riobárd Barton.

E. S. ó Dúgáin.

Seórsa Gabhán uí Dhúbhthaigh.

Signatories to the Anglo-Irish agreement of 1921

British troops leave Dublin after the signing of the treaty
Republic of Ireland representatives at the U.N. Assembly

State opening of the Northern Ireland Parliament
January 1965. Mr Sean Lemass and Captain Terence O'Neill meet in Belfast

O dear me the world's ill-divided,
Them that work the hardest are the least provided,
Shifting piece and spinning – warp, weft, and twine,
To feed and clothe my babies on ten and nine.[12]

Conditions like these seemed inevitable as people, transplanted from leafy lane to the squalor of cobbled street, reeled under the shock of the Industrial Revolution. Lung diseases and skin diseases in the flying flax dust were rife. Few grew old in those days. A doctor wrote:

When about thirty years old the appearance of the flax workers begins to alter, the face gets an anxious look, shoulders begin to get rounded – in fact they become prematurely aged and the greatest number die before forty-five years. . .[13]

The difference between the north-east corner and the rest of Ireland was now strikingly marked. An English traveller of the time commented:

It needs but a glance at Belfast and its surrounding country to perceive that the town and its neighbouring districts have nothing in common with the rest of Ireland.[14]

The Belfast area, different as it was from the rest of Ireland, was spreading its influence over much of Ulster. Whereas in the eighteenth century the main routes from the north all led to Dublin; by the year 1850 by far the most important route for trade was the one which ran from Belfast up the Lagan Valley to Armagh. And it was the importance of this Lagan Valley trade link that led to the first railway line being built in 1839 from Belfast to Lisburn. The merchants of Belfast had great faith in an east–west trade route across Ulster and they used money subscribed by Liverpool merchants to build a railway to Sligo.

At the same time as the modern road and railway systems were taking shape the increasing trade of the port of Belfast cried out for urgent expansion. In 1839 the channel of the river was straightened and by 1846 the port had deep water for big ships. Shipbuilding as an industry in the modern sense belongs to the second half of the nineteenth century, but it owes its foundation partly to the eighteenth century when a Scotsman, William Ritchie, had founded a small yard to supply Belfast merchants with their own ships. It is interesting to note from Wolfe Tone's diary of 1792:

I walked out with Henry Joy McCracken to see his brother's new ship the *Hibernia*. *Hibernia*, I was quick to notice, has got an English crown on her shield. We all roared at him.[15]

However, shipbuilding as we know it in Belfast today started strangely enough as an offshoot from linen from one of the many ironworks associated with linen manufacture in the town. In 1853 Robert Hickson started a shipyard as an outlet for the plates he manufactured at his Eliza Street Ironworks.

... The business has been commenced in a spirit that augurs well for its future success and importance, the vessels contracted for being of a very large tonnage and Mr Hickson already finding it necessary to ask for additional space.[16]

Mr Hickson's yard was soon acquired by his manager, Edward J. Harland, whose rapid development with his partner Wolff, soon created the biggest yard in the world. The engineering industry, which you remember had been initiated by the demand first for cotton and then linen machinery, expanded to meet the growing needs of the shipbuilders. And as the industry transcended these local needs it began to cater for world markets. The whole industrial scene of Belfast, a welter of linen mills, shipyards, engineering and ropeworks might seem an impossibility in a district that has been so purely agricultural.

Thomas Francis Meagher, in a speech he made in Belfast in the 1840s, commented on this.

I congratulate you, the citizens of Belfast, on escaping the ruin that has overtaken every other town in Ireland since the Act of Union. Your fate has been as singular as that of Robinson Crusoe and your ingenuity in making the most of a desert island has been no less remarkable.[17]

But Belfast in a way did not belong to the rest of the island. In 1843, Mr and Mrs Hall, the English travellers, wrote:

The cleanly and bustling appearance of Belfast is decidedly un-national. That it is in Ireland but not of it is a remark ever on the lips of visitors from the south or west.[18]

There is no doubt that from the seventeenth century onwards there were many differences between the north-east and the rest of the country. These differences were made stronger by the arrival of the Industrial Revolution. The Industrial Revolution not only increased the prosperity of Ulster but also linked it more closely with industrial Britain. But in the rest of Ireland poverty and depression still remained accompanied by political discontent. In this situation a new leader appeared and next week you will hear about his career – his name was Charles Stewart Parnell.

NOTES

1 Great Britain: Public Record Office *Calendar of Treasury Papers, 1702–1707* Longmans, and others. 1874. Introduction, p. 20.

2 Extract from a poem by Joseph Carson of Kilpike, near Banbridge (*circa* 1820).

3 Extract from a poem by Edward Sloan of Crawfordsburn (*circa* 1850).

4 Smith, F. W. *The Irish linen trade handbook and directory* Belfast: Greer, 1876. p. 46.

5 *Belfast News-Letter* June 1739.

6 Dubourdieu, Rev. J. *Statistical survey of Antrim* 2 pts. Dublin: Royal Dublin Society, 1812. p. 405.

7 Beggs, T. (1789–1847) *Auld wife's address to her spinning wheel*, a poem in Beggs, T. *Poetical works* Ballyclare: S. Corry, n.d. pp. 14–17.

8 Pim, J. *The conditions and prospects of Ireland* Dublin: Hodges and Smith, 1848. p. 70.

9 Lewis, S. *A topographical dictionary of Ireland* Lewis, 1837.

10 Quoted in *Ulster since 1800, a political and economic survey*; ed. by T. W. Moody and J. C. Beckett. BBC, 1954. p. 34.

11 *Belfast News-Letter* 1 May 1854.

12 Anonymous, *circa* 1860. Published by Mills Music Publications, London.

13 Purdom, C. D. *The sanitary states of the Belfast factory district during ten years, 1864–1873* Belfast: Adair, 1877.

14 Inglis, H. D. *Ireland in 1834: a journey throughout Ireland in the spring, summer and autumn of 1834* 2 vols. Whittaker, 1835.

15 Tone, W. T. W., ed. *Life of Theobald Wolfe Tone; written by himself . . . edited by his sons* 2 vols. Washington: Gales and Seaton, 1826. vol. 1, p. 172.

16 Belfast Harbour Commissioners *Report* 1853.

17 Quoted in Moody, T. W. and Beckett, J. C., eds. *Ulster since 1800* op. cit. p. 37.

18 Hall, S. C. and A. M. *Ireland: its scenery, character, etc.* 3 vols. How, 1841. vol. 3, p. 56.

6

PARNELL AND GLADSTONE

Bill Meek

Summary

DESPITE INCREASED industrial prosperity, most of Ireland remains agricultural and economically depressed. There is growing resentment towards landlords over high rents and evictions. The belief that justice will come only if Ireland's connection with Great Britain is severed – at least to some degree – becomes widespread. In 1870 a Home Government Association is formed by Isaac Butt to obtain an Irish parliament to legislate on Irish affairs.

At the age of twenty-nine Charles Stewart Parnell takes his seat at Westminster as a Home Ruler (1875). As a Protestant landlord of an old and distinguished Anglo-Irish family he is perhaps an unlikely potential leader of the struggle for the rights of the Irish peasantry. He has, however, been influenced by his American mother's overt hatred of England.

In parliament Parnell perfects the weapon of obstruction to focus attention on Irish grievances. His popularity in Ireland consequently grows and he soon ousts Butt from the leadership of the Irish Party. He makes alliances with the militant 'Fenian' movements in America and Ireland and with the Land League (founded in 1879 by Michael Davitt). The struggles for Home Rule and for better conditions on the land become closely associated. Under Parnell's presidency the Land League becomes strong and 'boycotts' those who side with the landlords. Parnell's defiance of Gladstone's Coercion Act leads to a term of imprisonment and, when he is released, to increased popularity in Ireland. In 1855 Parnell is the leader of eighty-six Home Rulers in Parliament and has the balance of power between the Liberals and the Conservatives. Gladstone (leader of the Liberals) converts to a policy of limited self-government for Ireland. His Home Rule Bill of 1886 is however defeated partly as a result of a split in the Liberal ranks. When Parnell is named as co-respondent in a divorce suit, Gladstone makes Parnell's resignation as leader of the Irish Party a condition of continued Liberal support for Home Rule. Parnell submits to pressure from the Liberals, the Roman Catholic hierarchy and also from his own party, and resigns. In 1891, at the age of forty-five, he dies having failed to reunite the nationalist movement.

Gladstone, for nearly twenty years before his first Home Rule Bill, has declared his intention to 'pacify Ireland'. In 1892, after Parnell's death, he becomes Prime Minister again and sets about introducing a second Home Rule Bill. In 1893 it is passed by the Commons but rejected by the Lords and, after this, Gladstone retires from public life.

a maid watched a boat on the waters that bore
To England the Chieftain of old Granuaile,
And cried in the bloom of her beauty once more
God prosper the Blackbird of Sweet Avondale.

At his voice the bolts of coercion will strain,
The lion in his den he will shortly assail,
Let all who wish freedom for Ireland again,
Remember the Blackbird of Sweet Avondale.[1]

You have heard in recent weeks how the population of Ireland was reduced by starvation, disease and emigration during the years of the great famine in the late 1840s. You have also heard how parts of Ireland underwent what was termed an Industrial Revolution. Despite the end of the famine and the new industrial boom most of the people continued to lead poverty-stricken lives as tenants of powerful landlords. If a tenant was unable to meet his rent he became liable to eviction. One who witnessed the eviction of a widow and her family was a journalist attached to the *Derry Standard*.

The bereaved widow and her daughters were frantic with despair. Throwing themselves on the ground they became almost insensible, and bursting out in the old Irish wail . . . their terrifying cries resounded along the mountainside for many miles. . . There these poor starving people remain on the cold bleak mountains, no one carying for them whether they live or die. 'Tis horrible to think of, but more horrible to behold.[2]

Because of such incidents resentment increased amongst the people. Many still entertained the notion, originally brought forward by the United Irishmen at the end of the previous century, that the only way to obtain justice for their country was to sever the connection with Great Britain, at least to some degree. One group, known as the Fenians, of whom you will hear more next week, tried unsuccessfully to raise an armed rebellion. Others placed their hopes on the Irish Members of Parliament in Westminster.

In 1870 a Home Government Association for Ireland was formed with this object:

> To obtain for our country the right and privilege of managing our own affairs by a Parliament assembled in Ireland, composed of Her Majesty, the Sovereign, and her successors, and the Lords and Commons of Ireland. To secure for that Parliament the right of legislating for and regarding all matters relating to the internal affairs of Ireland.[3]

It seemed to many that if the Irish members were to press for Home Rule they would have to submit themselves to a powerful leadership. This leadership was eventually provided by a young man elected as a Home Ruler for County Meath in 1875. When he took his seat he was only twenty-nine years of age. His name was Charles Stewart Parnell.

Parnell came from a very different background to that of Daniel O'Connell, yet like O'Connell he was to become the hero and even the idol of the Irish peasantry. He owned a large estate at Avondale in County Wicklow. He was an officer in the local militia, a synodsman of the Church of Ireland and had served as High Sheriff for his country. At no time had he really worked for his living. His career at Cambridge had been short and far from distinguished and generally his youth had been spent in the pleasant pursuits of the wealthy young squire. He rode to the hounds, played cricket with great enjoyment, if without skill, and loved to attend parties. Yet despite this background he was to become feared as a dangerous man by the same high society in which he had revelled.

Parnell, as a child, had been influenced by his mother, who was American, and who had feelings towards England that verged on hatred. When she arrived in Wicklow as a young bride she made no secret of her intense political feelings. Members of the family were alarmed and Parnell's great aunt wrote at the time:

> There is mischief brewing! I am troubled at what is going on at Avondale. My nephew's wife has a hatred of England and is educating her son, like a little Hannibal, to hate it too.[4]

In Parliament, Parnell found that he had little sympathy with most of his fellow Irish members. Although a majority of them favoured some form of Home Rule, few of them pursued this aim with much energy. The most colourful exception was Joseph Gillis Biggar, who was by trade a Belfast pork butcher and who often shocked his fellow members with his blunt manner of speech. A journalist wrote at the time:

Mr Biggar brings the manner of his store into this illustrious assembly, and his manner, even for a Belfast store, is very bad. When he rises to address the House, a whiff of salt pork seems to float upon the gale, and the air is heavy with the odour of the kippered herring.[5]

And yet Parnell chose to ally himself with the pork butcher and his friends. Partly to gain a hearing, and partly for nuisance value, they perfected a parliamentary weapon known as obstruction. That is by skilful debate, questioning and amendment they managed to hold up the business of the House to such an extent that Members were often forced to attend all-night sittings. The English papers were soon casting a jaundiced eye on the Member for Meath:

Mr Biggar, though occasionally endurable, is invariably grotesque; but Mr Parnell has no redeeming qualities. Unless we regard it as an advantage to have in the House one who united in his own person all the childish unreasonableness, the ill-regulated suspicion, and all the childish credulity of the Irish peasant, without any of the humour, the courtliness, or dash of the Irish gentleman.[6]

In Parliament Parnell infuriated the British Government. At home in Ireland he was received with tremendous enthusiasm by the people.

I believe that the maintenance of the class of landlords in a country is not for the general benefit of the greatest number. Ireland has suffered more than any country in the world from the maintenance of such a class. What must we do to induce the landlords to see the position? You must show the landlords that you intend to hold a firm grip of your homesteads and your land.[7]

Shortly afterwards, the Irish National Land League was founded:

To bring about the reduction of rack rents and to facilitate the obtaining of the ownership of the soil by the occupiers.[8]

The President of the League was Parnell. He began to concern himself increasingly with the problems of the small farmer and of the land. In County Clare he made a significant speech:

What are you to do to a tenant who bids for a farm from which another tenant has been evicted? I think I heard someone say shoot him. I wish to point out to you a very much better way – a more christian and charitable way, which will give the lost man an opportunity of repenting. When a man takes a farm from which another has been evicted you must shun him in the streets of the town, you must shun him in the shop, you must shun him in the fair green and in the market place, and even in the place of worship.[9]

One result of this speech was that when Lord Erne's agent refused a tenant's demand for reduced rent his servants deserted him, shopkeepers refused to provide him, and no one in the district would as much as speak to him. The agent's name was Captain Boycott – and a new word found its way into the dictionary.

Eighteen eighty was an important year for Parnell. A majority of the Home Rule members, that is those who wanted Ireland to be governed by an Irish Parliament, supported his methods and soon he became undisputed leader of the Irish Party. Many regarded him as leader of the Irish race.

Meanwhile, agitation continued to grow in Ireland and to cope with it the then Prime Minister, William Ewart Gladstone, through the Chief Secretary, W. E. Forster – known amongst the Irish as 'Buckshot' – introduced a coercion act which provided for the imprisonment of suspected persons without trial.

Gladstone was more than willing to make concessions to Irish demands but he was anxious to curb the lawlessness and violence generated by the agitation of the Land League. When the Coercion Act became law, Parnell defied it by actively encouraging the Land League to hold firm. But within a short time warrants were issued for the arrest of fourteen of its leaders. Amongst those subsequently imprisoned was Parnell.

> It was the tyrant Buckshot who said unto himself
> I never will be aisy till Parnell is on the shelf
> So make a warrant out in haste and send it by the Mail
> And we'll clap the pride of Erin's Isle in Could Kilmainham Gaol.[10]

But the effect of imprisoning Parnell was not to pacify Ireland. Indeed it was just the opposite. A new wave of discontent swept the country. The Government eventually decided that to release the Land Leaguers would be a positive step towards restoring order and in Kilmainham Gaol an unofficial treaty was negotiated. The Irish leaders agreed that in return for their release they would use their influence to help curb violence in the country. Furthermore, the Government promised an act of Parliament to assist tenants unable to pay their rent.

Parnell was released from gaol in May 1882 after serving six months.

Now the two major political parties in the British Parliament were the Conservatives and the Liberals. Parnell's Home Rule Party provided a small but important third force whose support of either one of the big two could diminish the power of the other. Parnell had therefore considerable bargaining power, especially with the Liberal leader, Gladstone, who, in spite of his coercion of Ireland, was sympathetic to many of her grievances.

In the general election of 1885, Parnell's party won a majority among Irish members. Gladstone again became Prime Minister, and in 1886 with Parnell's support he introduced a *Home Rule for Ireland* Bill. But Gladstone's own party was not united on the issue and the bill was defeated in the House of Commons. Despite this defeat of Home Rule in Parliament, Parnell's influence in Ireland grew stronger and even in Britain his prestige rose. But his power was not to last for long.

One of Parnell's party, a Captain William Henry O'Shea, filed divorce proceedings against his wife and named Parnell as the co-respondent. The charge was not denied, indeed after the divorce was granted, Parnell and Katherine O'Shea were married. Despite this harmful publicity the Irish Party met and reaffirmed its faith in the leader. But shortly afterwards a letter written by Mr Gladstone was made public.

The continuance of Mr Parnell at the present moment in the leadership of the Irish party would render my retention of the leadership of the Liberal Party, based as it has been mainly on the prosecution of the Irish cause, almost a nullity.[11]

In effect Gladstone suggested that if the Liberal Party were to continue to promote the cause of Home Rule, Parnell must go. Likewise a number of Roman Catholic bishops raised the moral issue and pronounced that Parnell should resign. A further meeting of the Irish Party was held and this time Parnell found a majority opposed to his continuing as leader. At once, without regard for his comfort or health, he started a series of exhausting trips around Ireland to try and gather support. But the old unity was gone and those who had previously formed a single Home Rule Party were now Parnellites or anti-Parnellites.

In the beginning of October 1891 Parnell became very ill, and on the seventh of that month he died in Brighton at the age of forty-five. His remains were brought to Dublin, and as the funeral procession of one hundred and fifty thousand persons marched to Glasnevin Cemetery there was little doubt as to the love that Irish people felt for their lost leader.

But the death of Parnell did not mean the death of the Home Rule Movement despite the fact that the Irish Party in Parliament had become hopelessly divided. It might seem surprising that the most energetic action towards the goal of Home Rule came from the Englishman, William Ewart Gladstone. All the more surprising when it is remembered that Gladstone had once agreed to the imprisonment of Parnell, and had been partially responsible for his downfall. And yet not surprising, because it was Gladstone who, in 1881, ten years before Parnell's death, had, with his Land Act, greatly improved the lot of the Irish tenant farmer. And it was Gladstone who, as far back as 1868, had declared:

My mission is to pacify Ireland.[12]

And it was Gladstone who had joined forces with the Irish leader to introduce the Home Rule Bill. Despite the fact that Parliament refused to pass it the Grand Old Man, as Gladstone was known by his friends, continued to press for some measure of independence for Ireland. Indeed, he devoted his life to those who suffered deprivation, and Ireland had a special place in his conscience.

As early as 1845 he wrote to his wife expressing a desire to give up politics, but for one thing:

Ireland! Ireland! That cloud in the west! That coming storm! The minister of God's retribution upon cruel injustice![13]

In 1892, after a number of years spent as leader of the opposition, Gladstone once again became Prime Minister. He immediately set about introducing a second Home Rule Bill. Both in Parliament and throughout the country his proposal met with spirited opposition. This opposition was particularly strong amongst Irish Unionists who saw the possibility of a Dublin Parliament as a threat to their whole way of life. Indeed, throughout Great Britain and Ireland as a whole, passions ran high over the subject of Home

Rule. Gladstone was faced with hostility by some of the most influential of his fellow countrymen. But in one of his speeches he said:

What is the case of Ireland at this moment? Have honourable gentlemen considered that they are coming into conflict with a nation? Can anything stop a nation's demand; in our opinion there is but one question before us in this demand. It is the time and circumstances of granting it. There is no question in our minds that it will be granted. Go into the length and breadth of the world, ransack the literature of all countries, find if you can a single voice, a single book in which the conduct of England towards Ireland is treated except with profound and bitter condemnation.[14]

At last, in 1893, the House of Commons passed the Home Rule Bill. There was jubilation amongst Liberals and Nationalists. But this jubilation was short-lived.

When the Bill came before the House of Lords it was rejected by 419 votes to 49. Gladstone shortly retired never to return to public life. But not all Irishmen were content with Gladstone's benevolent attitude towards their country. As you have heard the Irish Unionists, if anything, considered him a greater menace than Parnell. Others believed that the only hope of justice from England lay in taking up the gun against England, while many looked back regretfully to the golden days when Charles Stewart Parnell was uncrowned King of Ireland.

> He dared mankind to set the bounds to the nation marching on,
> The uncrowned King comes from the grave to lead the Irish throng,
> The Monarchs tremble on their thrones, they hear the passing knell,
> To set us free in majesty, did God restore Parnell.[15]

NOTES

1 *The blackbird of sweet Avondale* Anonymous.

2 *The Derry Standard* 8 April 1865.

3 Objects of the Home Government Association for Ireland, quoted in O'Hegarty, P. S. *A history of Ireland under the Union, 1801–1922. With an epilogue . . . to 1927* Methuen, 1952. p. 467.

4 Quoted in Cobbe, F. P. *Life of Frances Power Cobbe by herself* Bentley, 1894.

5 *The World* 5 March 1876.

6 Ibid. 29 March 1876.

7 Speeches of Mr Parnell quoted in the Times *Report of the proceedings before the Special Commission (1888–9)* 4 vols. *Times* 1890.

8 Resolutions establishing the Irish National Land League, 21 October 1879.

9 Speeches of Mr Parnell quoted in the Times *Report of the proceedings before the Special Commission (1888–9)* 4 vols. *Times* 1890.

10 Anonymous, *circa* 1882.

11 Quoted in Morley, J. *Life of William Ewart Gladstone* 3 vols. Macmillan, 1903.

12 Quoted in Beckett, J. C. *A short history of Ireland* Hutchinson, 1952. p. 162.

13 Magnus, Sir P. *Gladstone: a biography* Murray, 1954.

14 In the House of Commons. Quoted in Gladstone, W. E. *Speeches and public addresses. . .*; ed. by A. W. Hutton and H. J. Cohen. vols. 9 and 10. Methuen, 1892–4.

15 Anonymous *circa* 1895.

7

FENIAN AND SINN FEIN

Bill Meek

Summary

MANY OF THE Irish who emigrate to America during and after the Famine plan to revenge the wrongs they feel England has done to their country. Irish Americans play an important part in the American Civil War and after the war many resolve to use their military skill in the cause of Ireland against England. Meanwhile, Jeremiah O'Donovan Rossa under the cloak of 'The Phoenix Literary and Debating Society' forms a militant revolutionary organization in County Cork. In 1858 the Irish Republican Brotherhood is founded under James Stephens to co-ordinate the Irish and American revolutionary movements. The members call themselves 'Fenians' at the suggestion of John O'Mahony. The Fenians demand complete separation of Ireland from England.

Fenianism grows amongst Irish immigrants in Britain and the United States. In 1866 armed Fenians invade Canada but are repulsed. In 1867 there is a rising in Kerry with some American-

Fenian support but it is quickly put down. Various 'outrages' in British cities fail to further the Fenian cause directly but succeed in making the British public aware of the Irish nationalist mood.

The wish to be separate from England takes forms other than revolutionary. Dr Douglas Hyde forms the Gaelic League to revive the Irish language and promote Irish culture. In 1884 the Gaelic Athletic Association is formed by Dr Croke to promote Irish games. Irish brigades fight for the Boers against the British in South Africa.

In 1908, under Arthur Griffith, a number of separatist groups combine to form the 'Sinn Fein' organization. It advocates non-co-operation with Britain, the boycott of English goods, abstention from Parliament, and separate courts of law and civil service.

> 'Twas down by the glenside, I met an old woman,
> A plucking young nettles, she ne'er saw me comin',
> I listened a while to the song she was hummin',
> Glory O, Glory O, to the bold fenian men.
>
> When I was a young girl, their marching and drilling,
> Awoke in the glenside sounds awesome and thrilling,
> They loved poor Ireland, to die they were willing,
> Glory O, Glory O, to the bold fenian men.[1]

Last week you heard of the move to introduce Home Rule for Ireland by way of the Parliament at Westminster. However, during the lifetimes and after the deaths of Parnell and Gladstone there were many Irishmen who had no confidence in Parliament, and who felt that independence could be won only by force. Such were the beliefs of the Fenian Brotherhood.

> Some died by the glenside, some died with the stranger,
> And wise men have told us their cause was a failure,
> But they loved old Ireland and never feared danger,
> Glory O, Glory O, to the bold fenian men.

During the years of the great famine thousands of able-bodied Irishmen left their own country to settle in the United States. There they entered fully into the life of their new country but many of them did not forget the land of their birth and planned to revenge the wrongs they felt that England had done to it.

In 1861 a terrible civil war broke out between the north and south of the United States. In the Federal army, that is the army of the North, one of the most famous regiments, The City of New York 69th Volunteers, was composed entirely of Irishmen from the commander, General Meagher, down to the most junior private. Irishmen were also to be found in the southern or Confederate forces. One New York newspaper correspondent was vividly impressed at the extent of Irish participation in the war:

On the night of the bloody battle of Fredericksburgh, the Federal army lay sleepless and watchful on their arms, with spirits damped by the loss of so many gallant comrades. To cheer his brother officers Captain Downing sang his favourite song. The chorus of the first stanza was taken up by his dashing regiment, next by the brigade, next by the division, then by the entire line of the army for six miles along the river.[2]

> *Deep in Canadian Woods we've met,*
> *From one bright island flown,*
> *Great is the land we tread, but yet*
> *Our hearts are with our own.*
> *And ere we leave this shanty small,*
> *While fades the autumn day,*
> *We'll toast to Ireland, dear old Ireland,*
> *Ireland, boys, hurrah!*
>
> *Ireland, boys, hurrah,*
> *Ireland, boys, hurrah,*
> *We'll toast old Ireland, dear old Ireland,*
> *Ireland, boys, hurrah.*

And when the Captain ceased it was to listen with indefinable feelings to the chant that came like an echo from the Confederate lines on the opposite shore:[2]

> *Ireland, boys, hurrah,*
> *Ireland, boys, hurrah,*
> *We'll toast old Ireland, dear old Ireland,*
> *Ireland, boys, hurrah.*

After the war concluded many of these soldiers decided that they should find a way to use their military experience against British rule in Ireland. Even before the American civil war a group of young men who had not emigrated began to think in terms of armed resistance. Jeremiah O'Donovan Rossa formed *The Phoenix Literary and Debating Society* in Skibbereen, County Cork.

Outwardly the society appeared to be no more than a discussion group interested in questions touching on Irish nationalism. However at night the young members would take to the mountains and there practise drilling and the use of firearms. Before long many such groups were organized throughout the south. Writers in the Dublin papers became alarmed:

The members of the Societies bind themselves not to divulge their plans to the priests, and when spoken against from the altar they denounce the priests as despots. They are supposed to derive inspiration from America and money also. They declare their intention to rise in arms whenever there may be any difference with France or America. The Government is, I believe, aware of these facts.[4]

A move was started to co-ordinate the efforts of the Irish in America who favoured violent means and those at home who thought the same way, and so in 1858 the *Irish Republican Brotherhood* was founded.

James Stephens was appointed *Head Central Organizer for the Irish Revolution*.

At the suggestion of John O'Mahony, an Irish American leader, the members of the movement called themselves Fenians – the name given to the legendary warriors of ancient Ireland. Both Stephens and O'Mahony had taken part in the Young Ireland rebellion of 1848 after which they had been in exile in Paris at that time the centre of revolutionary movements throughout Europe. The Fenians demanded much more of Britain than Home Rule. They insisted on complete separation, and each member took a solemn oath:

I, in the presence of Almighty God, do solemnly swear allegiance to the Irish Republic and I will do my very utmost, while life lasts, to defend its independence and integrity; I will yield implicit obedience in all things, not contrary to the laws of God, to the commands of my superior officers. So help me God.[5]

In Ireland, England and the United States, Fenian organizers prepared for revolution. Thousands of Irishmen in the British Army took the oath and stood ready to desert to the rebel cause. The increase in Fenianism was viewed with growing concern by members of the Irish Roman Catholic clergy; but none were more vehement in their denunciation of the secret society than Dr Moriarty, Bishop of Kerry.

Hell is not hot enough nor eternity long enough to punish the Fenians.[6]

In 1865, four leading Fenians, O'Leary, Luby, O'Donovan Rossa and Stephens were arrested. Stephens, however, made a dramatic escape on the eve of his trial and managed to make his way to the United States. There he announced that 1866 was to be 'the year of victory'. In America a group of Fenians formed themselves into an armed band and invaded Canadian territory.

After initial successes they were repulsed by British troops and forced back to the United States.

The whole Fenian movement suffered from lack of good leadership and there was disagreement in the ranks as to the right moment to raise rebellion. It must also be remembered that the bulk of Irish people were indifferent or hostile to the Fenians.

In Ireland 'the year of victory' passed without a shot being fired. But in 1867 hostilities at last became open. A ship called the *Erins Hope*, manned by Fenians, sailed from Boston and a few men and guns were landed on Irish soil. However, the Fenian man-of-war made but one voyage.

> *Down by Boston Corner I carelessly did stray,*
> *I overheard a sailor lad who to his love did say,*
> *Bridget, dearest Bridget, from you I must go far,*
> *To fight against the cruel John Bull on the Fenian Man O War*[7]

The Fenian uprising was almost a total fiasco, due mainly to lack of co-ordination. In West Kerry Fenians took up arms in February and managed to harrass Government forces for a few weeks.

Elsewhere the rising took place in March. Despite the fact that thousands of Fenians turned out to fight, the rebellion was easily put down due to lack of arms, conflicting orders, and an unforeseen blizzard that completely disorganized Fenian plans.

In England the Fenian campaign was no more successful. An attempt to raid the arsenal of Chester Castle failed, and sometime later the two leading Fenians in England, Colonel Kelly and Captain Deasy, were arrested. A plan was formed to engineer their escape and a prison-van in which they were being transported through Manchester was attacked. The Fenians managed to rescue Kelly and Deasy, but in blowing open the van door they killed a policeman. The rescuers, Allen, Larkin and O'Brien, were themselves captured and, despite their claim that the killing was accidental, they were tried and hanged for murder.

> *One cold November morning in eighteen sixty seven,*
> *These martyrs to their country's cause a sacrifice were given,*
> *'God save Ireland' was their cry, all through the crowd it ran,*
> *The Lord have mercy on the boys that helped to smash the van.*[8]

From the dock the condemned men had cried:

God save Ireland.

The phrase was taken up by a poet and soon nationalist Irish-men were singing a new unofficial anthem:

> *God save Ireland, said the heroes,*
> *God save Ireland, said they all.*
> *Whether on the scaffold high,*
> *Or the battle field we die,*
> *O, what matter when for Ireland dear we fall.* [9]

Despite their failure the Fenians were the main inspiration of future generations of Irishmen who believed in the total separation of Ireland from the United Kingdom. But the wish to be separate from England took forms other than revolutionary. Many Irish-men felt that their country had become completely anglicized – Irishmen spoke English, read English books and newspapers, played English games, followed English customs in every way. They wanted to change all this, and restore what they regarded as the ancient Gaelic way of life. Language became a key issue.

At the beginning of the nineteenth century a large number of the Irish people spoke Gaelic, the native Irish language. By the last quarter of that century Gaelic was spoken only in certain remote areas, notably Donegal, Connaught, the south-west and parts of County Waterford.

A number of people feeling that the loss of the Irish language amounted to the loss of Irish nationality, decided to embark on a strenuous effort to revive the language and for this purpose formed a society called in Irish, *Connradh na Gaedhilge*, or in English, The Gaelic League. The League was presided over by Dr Douglas Hyde, a well-known classics scholar of Trinity College, Dublin.

If we take a bird's eye view of our island today and compare it with what it used to be, we must be struck with the extraordinary fact that the nation which was once as everyone admits, one of the most classically learned and cultivated nations in Europe, is now one of the least so.

I should like to call attention to the illogical position of men who drop their own language to speak English, of men who translate their euphoni-ous Irish names into English monosyllables, of men who read English books, and know nothing about Gaelic literature, nevertheless protesting as a matter of sentiment that they hate the country which at every hand's turn they rush to imitate. [10]

The policy of separateness from Britain was warmly supported by the Archbishop of Cashel, Dr Croke.

One of the most painful and at the same time, one of the most frequently recurring reflections that, as an Irishman, I am compelled to make is that we are daily importing from England her fashions, her accents, her vicious literature, her music, her dances, and her manifold mannerisms, her games also and her pastimes, to the utter discredit of our own great national sports.[11]

The Gaelic Athletic Association was founded in 1884 to promote Irish games, especially hurling and Gaelic football, and athletics. Thousands of young people joined the association, although Government spokesmen were not all happy about the movement. An eminent member of the Royal Irish Constabulary wrote of the association:

The underlying idea was the physical fitness of the youth of the nation as a preparation for achieving political independence by physical force methods. In athletics its activities were principally remarkable for the savagery of the games played. In politics the young braves have shown the same delight in violence.[12]

At the end of the nineteenth century Britain was at war. The scene of battle was South Africa where the British army was engaged in a bitter struggle with the Boers – South Africans of Dutch descent – under their Presidents Kruger and Steyn.

Irish regiments distinguished themselves, fighting courageously for the Empire; but other Irishmen, believing that a blow against the Empire no matter where in the world was a blow for Ireland, organized forces to fight in South Africa against the British – the chief of them an Irish Brigade led by Major John MacBride.

Throughout Ireland there was strong pro-Boer feeling amongst nationalists and some lines written by Parnell's sister, Fanny, became popular.

> Now Christ thee save Paul Kruger.
> Now Christ thee save from harm.
> And may the God of Joshua
> Bear up thy strong right arm.
>
> May he defend the children
> Who kept the father's cause
> Who raised the ocean ramparts
> And bade the spoiler pause.[13]

It is not surprising that the movement for separation in Ireland found political expression. Many nationalists had little praise for the Home Rule so enthusiastically sought by John Redmond, now leader of the Irish Parliamentary Party at Westminster. One who demanded much more was a Dublin editor called Arthur Griffith:

Lest there might be a doubt in any mind, we will say that we accept the Nationalism of '98, '48 and '67 as the true nationalism and Grattan's cry *Live Ireland – perish the Empire!* as the watchword of patriotism.[14]

Griffith believed that independence would not be achieved by talking politics in London, but rather by taking direct action at home in Ireland.

In 1908, under the guidance of Griffith, a number of groups combined to form a new political organization called Sinn Fein. The words *Sinn Fein* translate into English as *we ourselves*, and this notion of self-sufficiency was the very heart of the movement.

The object of Sinn Fein is to re-establish the Independence of Ireland.[15]

The policy of Sinn Fein was a bold one. But it was not a policy of armed defiance of Britain. It advocated non-co-operation with Britain; that British rule should in fact be ignored; Irish members should cease to attend Parliament in London but instead meet in Dublin; a civil service completely independent of the British administration should be set up; Irishmen should cease to offer their services to the British army; they should wherever possible boycott English goods; a system of law courts should exercise justice in Ireland in defiance of the British courts; and even an Irish merchant navy should be founded to carry direct trade between Ireland and foreign nations. Griffith argued that this policy would undermine Britain's rule in Ireland.

Sinn Fein's belief that independence could by these means be won without bloodshed was expressed by one of the leading Irish American supporters of the movement:

It is because Ireland is today unable to overcome England on the battlefield that we preach the Sinn Fein policy.[16]

But elsewhere in Ireland there were many who did not subscribe to the policies of non-violence. In the North a massive movement was arising prepared to resist Separation or even Home Rule by any means, and amongst nationalists there was to be found a number of men and women who were prepared if necessary to go beyond the passive doctrines of Sinn Fein. One of the most notable was a young poet and schoolteacher called Patrick Pearse.

Let us work together and exact a good measure from the English. But if we are deceived there are those in Ireland, and I am one of them, who will counsel the Gael to have no further dealings with the English, but to answer them with the sword's edge.[17]

NOTES

1 Words by Peadar Kearney. Published by Walton's, Dublin.

2 *New York Irish People* 9 March 1867.

3 Words by T. D. Sullivan. Published by Walton's, Dublin.

4 *Evening Mail* 27 October 1858.

5 Quoted in O'Leary, J. *Recollections of Fenians and Fenianism* 2 vols. Downey, 1896.

6 Quoted in O'Connor, T. P. *The Parnell Movement with a sketch of Irish parties from 1843* Kegan Paul, 1886. p. 227.

7 Anonymous *circa* 1870.

8 Anonymous *circa* 1870.

9 Words by T. D. Sullivan. Published by Walton's, Dublin.

10 Hyde, D. *The necessity for de-Anglicising Ireland* in Duffy, Sir C. *The revival of Irish literature* Dublin: T. Fisher Unwin, 1894.

11 O'Sullivan, T. F. *Story of the G.A.A.* Dublin, 1916. pp. 9–10.

12 Pollard, H. B. C. *Secret societies in Ireland, their rise and progress* Allan, 1922.

13 Quoted in McCarthy, M. J. F. *Five years in Ireland, 1895–1900* Simpkin, 1901.

14 *The United Irishman* 4 March 1899.

15 *1908 Constitution of Sinn Fein.*

16 Henry, R. M. *The evolution of Sinn Fein* T. Fisher Unwin, 1920.

17 Gwynn, S. *John Redmond's last years* Arnold, 1919. pp. 63–64. Pearse's speech was delivered in Irish.

8

'ULSTER WILL FIGHT'

David Hammond

Summary

GLADSTONE believes that the union of England and Ireland is
sound only as long as it gives Ireland good government. His Act of
Disestablishment (of the Church of Ireland) in 1871 increases his
popularity generally in Ireland. His policy of Home Rule further
enhances his popularity but offends Protestant sentiment in Ulster.
Ulster Protestants are suspicious of the Roman Catholic Church
and fear that 'Home Rule is Rome rule'. They believe that their
future depends on union with Britain. This unionist policy is supported by the British Conservatives. As the idea of Home Rule
grows, unionism in Ulster becomes stronger. Even after the defeat
of the first Home Rule Bill the tension leads to serious rioting in
Belfast (1886).

Gladstone's second Home Rule Bill (1892) provokes widespread
and well-organized opposition in Ulster. Unionists are resolved to
resist Home Rule with force, but the defeat of the Bill in the Lords
makes force unnecessary. In 1912 the Liberals (under H. H.
Asquith) introduce Home Rule proposals which are certain to become law after 1914. Under Sir Edward Carson and Sir James
Craig anti-Home Rule feelings reach a climax in 1912 when
thousands of Ulstermen swear to defeat Home Rule 'using all
means which may be found necessary'. The Ulster Volunteer
Force is formed and gathers arms. The Government orders the
army at the Curragh to move into the north but is faced with
mutiny. The Ulster Volunteers then smuggle a huge consignment
of arms from Germany. Meanwhile, the Irish Volunteers are
formed in the south to dissolve the Union. In 1914 the Great War
breaks out, the Home Rule question hangs fire and thousands of
Irishmen fight side by side in Flanders.

*S*ir *Edward Carson had a cat,*
It sat upon the fender,
And every time it saw a mouse,
It shouted 'No surrender'.

He left it by the fireside,
Whenever he went away,
And when he returned he also found
It singing 'Dolly's Brae'.

You heard last week how the rise of Fenianism in Ireland brought a new spirit to Irish nationalism – a spirit of violence. You remember how this spirit suddenly exploded in the streets of English cities. The English people realized, probably for the first time, with a sense of shock and horror, the true and ugly nature of Irish affairs. The attention of the Westminster Parliament was riveted to Ireland and Gladstone, the Prime Minister, reflected the distress when he said:

The influence of Fenianism was this – when the tranquillity of Manchester was disturbed, when London itself was shocked by and terrified by an inhuman outrage, when a sense of insecurity went abroad far and wide, then the whole population realised the vast importance of the Irish controversy.[1]

Gladstone himself had always felt that the union between England and Ireland was sound only as long as it gave Ireland good government. As you have heard in previous speeches he was willing to offer Ireland that which Parnell and his Irish Party had long been seeking – Home Rule.

Gladstone's intention stirred Ulster to its depths. Ulster Unionists wanted to remain joined to Britain. It did not matter that Gladstone's plan for Home Rule would give Ireland little more than command over its own local affairs, self-government little more than in name.

From 1885 on, Ulster's faith in Gladstone's Liberal Party was wrecked. For the next thirty years, every time the Liberals were elected to power, Ulster had good reason to catch its breath for most of the people of that part of Ireland wanted nothing to do with Home Rule.

The Industrial Revolution had brought Ulster a prosperity unknown to the rest of Ireland, a prosperity linked to the industries and the markets of Britain. Break that link with Britain, the Ulster people reasoned, and you destroy the prosperity and reduce the northern province to the distress that tormented the rest of Ireland.

Irish nationalism had a predominantly Roman Catholic following. Ulster Protestants viewed the Roman Catholic Church with suspicion.

Home Rule is Rome Rule.

And above all Ulstermen were proud of the place they held in the British Empire at a time when that empire's power was at its zenith; they would resist any proposal that would rob them of that fierce pride. So as soon as Gladstone announced his intention to introduce a Home Rule Bill the Ulster Protestants threw their weight into a campaign to swing British public opinion in favour of the Ulster cause, to convince the British people that Ulstermen wanted to be British too.

The British Conservative Party was, of course, already opposed to the Liberal policies; Conservatives declared themselves totally for the Union and themselves took the name of Unionists. One of their leaders, Lord Randolph Churchill came hurrying to the Ulster Hall in Belfast to promise the Ulster Unionists the complete backing of the English Conservative Party. He said:

... the loyalists in Ulster should wait and watch – organize and prepare...[2]

They followed his advice. They wrote letters to newspapers, speakers rallied support on English and Scottish platforms, all making clear that Home Rule was a threat to the Empire and a stab in the back for loyal Ulster. The Orange Order, a somewhat disreputable body up until then, was given a new importance by Lord Randolph Churchill's remark.

... the Orange card is the one to play...[3]

And immediately the Orange Order became highly respectable and exceedingly powerful, for people of every class swelled its ranks – country gentlemen, Protestant clergymen, business men, tradesmen, labourers, farmers. They flaunted their sashes, as tokens of loyalty, their drums thundered defiance over the countryside, they vowed to preserve the Union and they chanted Lord Randolph Churchill's slogan as a war cry.

Ulster will fight, and Ulster will be right.[4]

In Ulster the idea of resisting the setting up of a Dublin parliament by force became a popular sentiment. But in 1886, as it turned out, no force, no illegal action was called for – the question of Home Rule was decided peacefully and constitutionally in the Westminster Parliament when the Home Rule Bill was defeated; Gladstone's own party, the Liberals, were themselves divided on the issue. So Parliament was dissolved and the Conservative Party won the new election. Ulster could breathe again.

But the high feeling that Gladstone's intention had provoked in Ulster in 1886 did not subside overnight. The tension that had been simmering uneasily in the streets of Belfast boiled over in the summer. There were serious riots between Protestant and Catholic workmen.

The month of June 1886 opened in Belfast upon a condition of great excitement and high party feeling. The Home Rule Bill was then before parliament and the measure evoked strong feeling in Belfast. The Catholics as a body supported the Bill – the Protestants regarded it with hostility; on Friday the scandalous outrage causing the death of the young lad, Curran; on Sunday the wanton rioting at Curran's funeral.[5]

Although Belfast gradually quietened down over thirty people died in the violence of that summer. To English people this was an ominous indication that the settlement of the Irish question would cost many lives.

In 1892, Ulster was forced to the alert again for Gladstone, still pledged to Home Rule, was re-elected Prime Minister. But on this occasion the Ulster Unionists were well fortified for the introduction of the Bill. Immediately they swung into attack, countless demonstrations were held throughout Ireland, the most memorable being the great Ulster convention in Belfast in 1892. Excitement grew high in the packed streets and nearly 12,000 delegates from all parts of the country carried this resolution.

We solemnly resolve and declare that we express the devoted loyalty of Ulster Unionists to the crown and constitution of the United Kingdom; that we avow our fixed resolve to retain unchanged our present position as an integral part of the United Kingdom; that we declare to the people of Great Britain our conviction that the attempt to set up such an all-Irish Parliament will result in disorder, violence and bloodshed.[6]

Here again was the alarming statement that the Ulster Unionists would resist Home Rule with physical force. Lord Randolph Churchill had planted his seed on fertile ground. The population cheered when Thomas Andrews, formerly a staunch Liberal, threatened:

... as a last resource we will be prepared to defend ourselves...[7]

But no violence was called for; although Gladstone pushed his second Home Rule Bill through the House of Commons the House of Lords rejected it in 1893. Ulster again had a space to get her breath back and make ready for future assaults on the union of Great Britain and Ireland.

Two years later, in 1895, the Conservatives were back in office. The Ulster Unionists were among friends again – and the Union was safe for the time being. Tension waned but the Unionists did not relax during the next ten years. Their whole effort was directed at uniting people of every class into one body. This single body with one voice was born in 1905 and was named the Ulster Unionist Council. It was only just in time too, for soon after, Conservative rule at Westminster ended and the Liberals were back in office. Home Rule for Ireland seemed now only a matter of time.

But, first of all, the Liberals before they attended to the Home Rule question decided to curb the power of the House of Lords once and for all. Never again would the House of Commons push a Bill through all its stages only to find it rejected by the House of Lords – on this the Liberals were determined. They achieved their aim and in 1912 when a Home Rule Bill was introduced it seemed as if nothing could stop it from becoming law.

Gladstone was dead but his soul was marching on. But the Ulster Unionist Council had also been on the march during all these seven years of menace from the Liberal commitment to Home Rule. They had taken as their leader in 1910 Sir Edward Carson. Carson was from Dublin, a southern Unionist and a lawyer. He had been a Member of Parliament for nearly twenty years and could gauge precisely the support he could expect from the English Unionists. He was an orator – no public speaker since Daniel O'Connell swayed Irishmen as Sir Edward Carson swayed the Unionists of Ulster. In 1911, a great demonstration was held near Belfast on the estate of another Unionist leader, James Craig.

Before a crowd of thousands Carson flatly laid it down that the Ulster Unionist Council would never accept Home Rule. Even if it did become law, Ulster would defy that law. These were strong words but Carson convinced his audience that this was their right. He spoke of plans to set up for Ulster its own provisional government.

We must be prepared the morning Home Rule passes, ourselves to become responsible for the government of the Protestant province of Ulster.[8]

The situation was serious. Here was a body representing most of the Protestant opinion of Ulster declaring its intention of defying the law of the land. Lord Londonderry said in the House of Lords:

I warn your Lordships that if a Home Rule Parliament is established there will be lawlessness, serious disorder and bloodshed. I want to warn the government what will occur.[9]

The English Unionists proclaimed themselves champions of the Ulster Unionists. Bonar Law, their leader, said at Larne in 1912:

I have only one more word to say, and that is, that if this Home Rule Bill should by any chance be forced through, then God help Ulster, but Heaven help the government that tries to enforce it.[10]

But talk of Government and Parliament had now become more and more like a fairy tale. Orangemen in Ulster had already started to drill in military style. And, more important, the feelings of resistance to Home Rule reached a climax in 1912 when nearly half a million Ulstermen signed a solemn league and covenant, swearing to defeat Home Rule, as they said, 'using all means which may be found necessary'.

All over Ulster on Saturday, 28 September 1912, Ulster Protestants flocked the roads to local centres to sign their names and attend religious services. In Belfast the scene was unforgettable – the shipyard was silent that Saturday.

Now there is not the sound of a hammer; all is as silent as the grave. The splendid craftsmen who build the largest ships in the world have donned their Sunday clothes, and with Unionists buttons on their lapels, or Orange sashes on their shoulders, are about to engage on what to them is an even more important task.[11]

And when Sir Edward Carson arrived at the City Hall the streets were jammed with his supporters. But instead of the usual hurricane of cheers the people expressed the deep emotion of the day by taking off their hats and greeting him in respectful silence.

Ulster's
Solemn League and Covenant.

Being convinced in our consciences that Home Rule would be disastrous to the material well-being of Ulster as well as of the whole of Ireland, subversive of our civil and religious freedom, destructive of our citizenship and perilous to the unity of the Empire, we, whose names are underwritten, men of Ulster, loyal subjects of His Gracious Majesty King George V., humbly relying on the God whom our fathers in days of stress and trial confidently trusted, do hereby pledge ourselves in solemn Covenant throughout this our time of threatened calamity to stand by one another in defending for ourselves and our children our cherished position of equal citizenship in the United Kingdom and in using all means which may be found necessary to defeat the present conspiracy to set up a Home Rule Parliament in Ireland. ¶ And in the event of such a Parliament being forced upon us we further solemnly and mutually pledge ourselves to refuse to recognise its authority. ¶ In sure confidence that God will defend the right we hereto subscribe our names. ¶ And further, we individually declare that we have not already signed this Covenant.

The above was signed by me at_____
"Ulster Day," Saturday, 28th September, 1912.

God Save the King.

Many men who signed the Solemn League and Covenant scorned the use of ink for a document that expressed the destiny of Ulster and signed in their own blood.

Being convinced in our consciences that Home Rule would be disastrous to the material well-being of Ulster as well as of the whole of Ireland, subversive of our civil and religious freedom, destructive of our citizenship . . . we stand by one another in defending for ourselves and our children our cherished position of equal citizenship in the United Kingdom and in using all means which may be found necessary to defeat the present conspiracy to set up a Home Rule parliament in Ireland. . .[12]

But still the Liberals persisted in pushing the Home Rule Bill through Parliament. A prominent Liberal of the time, Winston

Spencer Churchill, was seemingly unaware of the strength of feeling in Ulster. Early in 1912 he visited Belfast to persuade the local Unionists that they were wrong. He had completely misjudged Ulster feeling and he nearly paid for his mistake with his life. His safety during the brief stay was only guaranteed with the aid of five battalions of infantry and two squadrons of cavalry as well as the normal police force. But Winston Churchill was never easily frightened. Later that year he wrote:

The Ulster menace is nothing but melodramatic stuff and the Unionist leaders would be unspeakably shocked and frightened if anything came of their foolish and wicked words.[13]

But events in 1913 seemed to show that the Ulster menace was a very real thing. For Unionists had further declared their intention of resistance by forming the Ulster Volunteer Force and gathering together guns and ammunition. They were preparing to fight the British Government for not allowing them to remain within the Union and their slogans echoed throughout Ulster.

Ulster will fight and Ulster will be right.
No surrender. Remember 1690.

Asquith, the Liberal Prime Minister, could not reason with the Ulstermen whose attitudes were now regarded as rebellious. And so the Government, determined to break Ulster's resistance with a show of force, ordered the British Army stationed at the Curragh near Dublin to move into the north. But many of the officers resigned rather than take action against Ulster. The Ulster Unionists, on the other hand, may have been already confident that the British Army never would attack Ulstermen. At any rate, the very next month after the Curragh incident, the Ulster Volunteer Force of 100,000 members, smuggled mainly through Larne 35,000 German rifles and five million rounds of ammunition.

The arms were quietly distributed all over Ulster, under the noses of the police force and the army, and hidden ready for use in haystacks, farm kitchens and the backyards of terraced houses.

The Government was now in serious difficulty. There were 100,000 armed, determined Ulstermen facing them on one side, and on the other side stood John Redmond, successor to Parnell, and leader of the Irish Nationalist Party. Redmond was committed to obtaining Home Rule, but by purely peaceful means.

His great advantage was that without the support of his party the Liberal Government would fall.

But already John Redmond, who had seen Home Rule as a certainty, now saw his authority being threatened in Ireland by impatient groups who had lost faith in Britain's good intentions of Home Rule and who believed that force was the only way to independence. This movement towards force was accelerated in Dublin by the news of the gun-running at Larne and as a counterblast to the Ulster Volunteers crowds flocked into the drill halls of the Irish Volunteers.

It is important to remember that the two Volunteer movements were recruited to fight, not against each other, but against the British Government. But whereas the Ulster Volunteers sought to fight to maintain the union of Great Britain and Ireland, the Irish Volunteers were demanding the ending of that union.

The two leaders, Carson and Redmond, met in 1914 at a conference in Buckingham Palace but they could not reach any agreement. And then, just when it looked as if Ireland was on the brink of bloodshed, Britain and Europe were plunged into the First World War.

The granting of self-government to Ireland was postponed until such time as the war would end and thousands of Irishmen from north and south joined the British forces. Many enlisted in the belief that the Irish problem would be solved when the fighting was done. Others took to the battlefield that same fierce loyalty to Britain which had sustained their resistance to Home Rule.

On 1 July 1916 a correspondent from *The London Times* wrote about the Battle of the Somme:

When I saw the Ulstermen emerge through the smoke and form up as on parade, I could hardly believe my eyes. Then I saw them attack, beginning at a slow walk over no-man's land, and then suddenly let loose as they charged over the two front lines of the enemy's trenches, shouting 'No surrender'.

But in that same year, 1916, other Irishmen had thrown themselves into a desperate struggle in Ireland. They had not conceded, as John Redmond had, that Britain's struggle in the war was more important than Ireland's independence. They believed instead that England's weakness was Ireland's opportunity. Next week you will hear their story, the story of the Easter Rising.

1 Morley, J. *Life of William Ewart Gladstone* 3 vols. Macmillan, 1903. vol. 1, p. 654.

2 Speech in Ulster Hall, 22 February 1886. Quoted in Churchill, W. S. *Lord Randolph Churchill* 2 vols. Macmillan, 1906. vol. 2, p. 62.

3 Quoted in Inglis, B. *The story of Ireland* Faber 1956. p. 92.

4 In a letter from Lord Randolph Churchill, May 1886. Quoted in Moody, T. W. and Beckett, J. C. eds. *Ulster since 1800, a political and economic survey* BBC, 1964. p. 94.

5 Extract from the report of Belfast Riots Commission to the Lord Lieutenant of Ireland, 1886.

6 Extract from a resolution passed at the Ulster Unionist Convention in Belfast, 17 June 1892.

7 From a speech by Thomas Andrews, Ulster Convention, 19 June 1892.

8 From a speech by Sir Edward Carson, 23 September 1911.

9 From a speech in the House of Lords, 20 July 1911.

10 Easter Monday, 9 April 1912.

11 *The Standard* 30 September 1912.

12 Abridged from the Solemn League and Covenant published in Belfast in September 1912. A reproduction of the document appears on p. 101 of this book and also on p. 18 of the pupils' pamphlet.

13 Extract from a letter to a constituent in Scotland. Quoted in McNeill, R. *Ulster's stand for Union* Murray, 1922. p. 99.

9

THE EASTER RISING

G. A. Hayes-McCoy

Summary

BEFORE THE First World War many people in Ireland look forward to some form of Home Rule, but few think of setting up an Irish republic. Nevertheless, extreme nationalist elements are secretly preparing for revolution. In 1914 the Irish Republican Brotherhood (a revival of the Fenian movement founded in 1858) is actively recruiting, but John Redmond's Irish Parliamentary

Party is still the accepted voice of public opinion throughout most of Ireland.

In reaction to the Ulster Volunteer Force, the Irish Volunteers are formed and rapidly increase to seventy-five thousand. In July 1914 arms are smuggled from Germany. When the First World War breaks out, Sinn Fein, for one, resents Ireland's being involved, while the I.R.B. regards England's difficulty as Ireland's opportunity. The I.R.B. sets up a military council. Patrick Pearse is in charge and it includes James Connolly, the labour leader, who has helped to form a 'citizen army'. Preparations for a rising of volunteers and citizen army are kept secret from both the authorities and moderate nationalist leaders like Redmond and MacNeill (Chief of Staff of the Volunteers).

Sir Roger Casement negotiates for assistance from Berlin but the plan to supply further arms to the Irish rebels miscarries and Casement is captured. Rebellion nevertheless breaks out on Easter Monday 1916 and an Irish Republic is proclaimed. The fighting is confined mainly to Dublin and within a week the revolt is crushed. Sixteen leaders are executed, the main effect of their execution being that from being unpopular extremists they become heroes.

ITTLE MORE THAN fifty years ago people in Ireland, either north or south, thought of breaking the political connection with Britain and of setting up an independent Ireland. Many Irishmen, especially outside Ulster, looked forward to Home Rule in those days – yes; but to the removal of the crown from above the harp, to the setting up of an Irish Republic, to the splitting of Ireland in two – no.

Yet there were some who thought deeply about complete national sovereignty for Ireland and were prepared to fight – if necessary to die – to achieve it.

In 1914 these extremists were banded together in a secret revolutionary organization named the Irish Republican Brotherhood, the I.R.B. – the same Fenian Brotherhood that we heard about two weeks ago. While the world was still at peace the I.R.B., its activities hidden beneath everyday affairs, spread underground.

I do solemnly swear to obey the constitution of the Irish Republican Brotherhood, to do all in my power to assert the national independence of

105

Ireland, to obey the commands of my superior officers, and to keep secret the business of this organisation. So help me, God.[1]

In 1914 there were no more than two thousand I.R.B. men. In comparison with John Redmond's Irish Parliamentary Party who were the advocates of Home Rule and the acknowledged leaders of the vast majority of Irishmen, they were ridiculously weak. The contrast between them and the loyal supporters of the mighty British Empire, then at the height of its prestige and power

Oglaigh na hEireann.

ENROL UNDER THE GREEN FLAG.

Safeguard your rights and liberties (the few left you).

Secure more.

Help your Country to a place among the nations.

Give her a National Army to keep her there.

Get a gun and do your part.

JOIN THE

IRISH VOLUNTEERS

(President : EOIN MAC NEILL).

The local Company drills at_____

_____

Ireland shall no longer remain disarmed and impotent.

showed how absurd were their hopes of starting a revolution. Yet the I.R.B. was not without allies.

In November 1913, a group of Irishmen, impressed by the success of the Ulster Unionists in forming the Ulster Volunteer Force to resist Home Rule, had founded the Irish Volunteers with the very opposite purpose. Their object was to secure Irish liberties by uniting Irishmen in an armed voluntary association.

The Volunteers, although they were as yet largely unarmed, were an immediate success. By the summer of 1914 their strength was seventy-five thousand. Efforts made by Redmond to control them more than doubled their number, but real control over those who mattered, those who were in earnest in their determination to fight, was exercised neither by Redmond nor indeed by the Volunteer leaders, but by the Irish Republican Brotherhood.

The I.R.B. was in a position too to influence public opinion and to further its own ends through other bodies that had grown up in recent years – through Sinn Fein, the party, as you remember, that was led by Arthur Griffith to hasten Irish self-government and to make Ireland self-supporting; through the Gaelic League, which hoped to awaken interest in the culture of the past and to extend the use of the Irish language; and through the Gaelic Athletic Association, which encouraged Irish games and pastimes. The I.R.B. alone saw that if the Volunteers deserved arms they must be prepared to use them.

Arms were provided in July 1914. Over fifteen hundred German rifles and a supply of ammunition were landed in that month at Howth outside Dublin and at Kilcool in Wicklow and were distributed among the Volunteers in Dublin. As that lovely summer moved towards its tragic end, Irish restlessness increased.

> *I will sing you a song of peace and love,*
> *Whack fol the diddle lol the di do day,*
> *Of the land that rules all lands above,*
> *Whack fol the diddle lol the di do day.*
> *May peace and plenty be her share,*
> *Who kept our homes from want and care,*
> *Oh, God bless England is our prayer,*
> *Whack fol the diddle lol the di do day.*
>
> *Oh, Irishmen forget the past,*
> *Whack fol the diddle lol the di do day,*

And think of the day that is coming fast,
Whack fol the diddle lol the di do day,
When we shall all be civilized,
Neat and clean and well advised,
Oh, won't mother England be surprised,
Whack fol the diddle lol the di do day.

> *Whack fol the diddle lol the di do day,*
> *So we say – Hip hurrah,*
> *Come and listen while we pray,*
> *Whack fol the diddle lol the di do day.*[2]

The world was changing. The great nations of Europe had been at peace for two generations, but now in 1914 it seemed that violence would soon break out again. Austria, Germany, Russia, France, Britain slipped towards the brink of war. In August they toppled over. The good old days had ended and the First World War had begun.

The Irish, being citizens of the United Kingdom of Great Britain and Ireland, were of course at war too, but different Irishmen viewed the situation differently. John Redmond spoke:

I say to the government that they may tomorrow withdraw every one of their troops from Ireland. Ireland will be defended by her armed sons from foreign invasion, and for the purpose the armed Catholics in the south will be only too glad to join arms with the armed Protestant Ulstermen. Is it too much to hope that out of this situation a result may spring which will be good, not merely for the Empire, but for the future welfare and integrity of the Irish nation?[3]

But Arthur Griffith, the leader of Sinn Fein, disagreed:

Ireland is not at war with Germany. She has no quarrel with any continental power. England is at war with Germany, and Mr Redmond has offered England the services of the Volunteers to defend Ireland. What has Ireland to defend, and whom has she to defend it against?

Our duty is in no doubt. We are Irish Nationalists, and the only duty we can have is to stand for Ireland's interests, irrespective of the interests of England, or Germany, or any other foreign country.[4]

But the views of Redmond and Griffith were moderate compared with those of the I.R.B. For them the war was not unwelcome. They regarded England's difficulty as Ireland's opportunity. Patrick Pearse spoke for the I.R.B. when he said:

The European war has brought about a crisis which may contain, as yet hidden within it, the moment for which the generations have been waiting.

It remains to be seen whether, if that moment reveals itself, we shall have the sight to see and the courage to do; or whether it shall be written of this generation, alone of all the generations of Ireland, that it had none among it who dared to make the ultimate sacrifice.[5]

In the first weeks of war, while the British Army suffered severe setbacks in France, the I.R.B. resolved that a rising must take place against British rule in Ireland before the conflict was over. A Military Council was set up. Patrick Pearse, Eamon Kent and Joseph Plunkett were its first members, and they were joined by Tom Clarke, Sean MacDermott, Thomas MacDonagh and James Connolly. These were the men who organized the 1916 revolt.

Their task was difficult. They had to seek the assistance of Germany, the enemy of tens of thousands of their countrymen who had joined the British Army. Their preparations had to be kept secret, not alone from the British, to whom they were treason, but from their more moderate comrades. Eoin MacNeill, Chief-of-Staff of the Volunteers, and many others believed that the Volunteers should not provoke a struggle in which they were bound to be overcome. MacNeill's policy was to remain in arms in the hope that, when the war was ended, the Volunteers could successfully demand Home Rule.

So it was essential for the I.R.B., who were dependent on Volunteer support, to be able to complete their arrangements without MacNeill's knowledge and to be able, if necessary, to dispense with his control. Yet they themselves were doubly in danger of being forestalled; they were not the only Irish revolutionaries.

The labour unrest which had brought on the great strike in Dublin in 1913 had resulted in the formation of the Irish Citizen Army, a small but resolute force led by James Connolly. By the beginning of 1916, before the arrangements of the Military Council of the I.R.B. were complete, Connolly threatened a rising of his own, a rising of workers who wanted better social conditions and were prepared to fight for them.

The ability of Patrick Pearse and his comrades to overcome all these difficulties is the measure of their determination. Pearse's purpose hardened. He said at the graveside of the Fenian, O'Donovan Rossa:

Life springs from death; and from the graves of patriot men and women spring living nations.

The Defenders of this Realm have worked well in secret and in the open. They think that they have pacified Ireland. They think that they have purchased half of us and intimidated the other half. They think that they have foreseen everything, think that they have provided against everything; but the fools, the fools, the fools! – they have left us our Fenian dead, and while Ireland holds these graves, Ireland unfree shall never be at peace.[6]

In January 1916 Connolly and the I.R.B. reached agreement. A joint rising of the Volunteers and Citizen Army was planned to take place at Easter. Arms were sought from Germany through Irish agents in America. In February Count von Bernstorff, German Ambassador to the United States, passed the request to Berlin:

Irish leader, John Devoy, informs me rising to begin in Ireland Easter Saturday. Send arms to arrive west coast Ireland between Good Friday and Easter Saturday.[7]

But the plot miscarried. As Easter approached everything seemed to go wrong. The I.R.B. had intended that routine Volunteer manœuvres, openly planned for Easter Sunday, should in fact begin the revolt. In their deep scheme this mobilization would coincide with the arrival of the German rifles, and ten thousand – perhaps twenty thousand – men, suddenly armed, would stand revealed as insurgents.

On the Thursday before Easter MacNeill discovered Pearse's intention, and, as Chief-of-Staff, cancelled the manœuvres. On Good Friday he was led to change his mind, since he saw that the arrival of the German arms must precipitate a struggle and that they were all, moderates and extremists alike, involved.

But the arms did not arrive. The German steamer reached the agreed landing place in Tralee Bay before the expected time and was captured by a British naval vessel. Sir Roger Casement, who had been negotiating for assistance in Berlin, was put ashore from a German submarine and promptly arrested. On Saturday morning the steamer was scuttled by her crew. Twenty thousand rifles sank to the bottom of the sea.

MacNeill returned to his original position. On Easter Sunday Ireland read his final order in the newspaper:

Owing to the very critical position, all orders given to Irish Volunteers for tomorrow, Easter Sunday, are hereby rescinded and no parades, marches,

POBLACHT NA H EIREANN.

THE PROVISIONAL GOVERNMENT
OF THE
IRISH REPUBLIC
TO THE PEOPLE OF IRELAND.

IRISHMEN AND IRISHWOMEN : In the name of God and of the dead generations from which she receives her old tradition of nationhood. Ireland, through us, summons her children to her flag and strikes for her freedom.

Having organised and trained her manhood through her secret revolutionary organisation, the Irish Republican Brotherhood, and through her open military organisations, the Irish Volunteers and the Irish Citizen Army, having patiently perfected her discipline, having resolutely waited for the right moment to reveal itself, she now seizes that moment, and, supported by her exiled children in America and by gallant allies in Europe, but relying in the first on her own strength, she strikes in full confidence of victory.

We declare the right of the people of Ireland to the ownership of Ireland, and to the unfettered control of Irish destinies, to be sovereign and indefeasible. The long usurpation of that right by a foreign people and government has not extinguished the right, nor can it ever be extinguished except by the destruction of the Irish people. In every generation the Irish people have asserted their right to national freedom and sovereignty ; six times during the past three hundred years they have asserted it in arms. Standing on that fundamental right and again asserting it in arms in the face of the world, we hereby proclaim the Irish Republic as a Sovereign Independent State, and we pledge our lives and the lives of our comrades-in-arms to the cause of its freedom, of its welfare, and of its exaltation among the nations.

The Irish Republic is entitled to, and hereby claims, the allegiance of every Irishman and Irishwoman. The Republic guarantees religious and civil liberty, equal rights and equal opportunities to all its citizens, and declares its resolve to pursue the happiness and prosperity of the whole nation and of all its parts, cherishing all the children of the nation equally, and oblivious of the differences carefully fostered by an alien government, which have divided a minority from the majority in the past.

Until our arms have brought the opportune moment for the establishment of a permanent National Government, representative of the whole people of Ireland and elected by the suffrages of all her men and women, the Provisional Government, hereby constituted, will administer the civil and military affairs of the Republic in trust for the people.

We place the cause of the Irish Republic under the protection of the Most High God, Whose blessing we invoke upon our arms, and we pray that no one who serves that cause will dishonour it by cowardice, inhumanity, or rapine. In this supreme hour the Irish nation must, by its valour and discipline and by the readiness of its children to sacrifice themselves for the common good, prove itself worthy of the august destiny to which it is called.

Signed on Behalf of the Provisional Government,

THOMAS J. CLARKE,
SEAN MacDIARMADA,   THOMAS MacDONAGH,
P. H. PEARSE,   EAMONN CEANNT,
JAMES CONNOLLY.   JOSEPH PLUNKETT.

III

or other movements of Irish Volunteers will take place. Each individual Volunteer will obey this order strictly in every particular.[8]

But the I.R.B. would not be deterred. Early on Easter Monday morning came the call that many awaited. With or without help, with or without hope, the Military Council would fight.

Irishmen and Irishwomen: In the name of God and of the dead generations from which she receives her old tradition of nationhood, Ireland, through us, summons her children to her flag and strikes for her freedom...

We declare the right of the people of Ireland to the ownership of Ireland, and to the unfettered control of Irish destinies, to be sovereign and indefeasible.[9]

The proclamation of the Irish Republic took Britain – and Ireland – by surprise. Armed largely with the Howth rifles, over a thousand Volunteers and Citizen Army men seized prominent Dublin buildings on Easter Monday. They were unopposed. Pearse and Connolly established their headquarters in the General Post Office on the north side of the River Liffey. South of the river the rebels threatened Dublin Castle, the centre of the British administration.

But after their first flourish they could do no more than hold their ground. Isolated risings in Galway, Wexford and north Dublin did little to help them.

The British crushed the rising methodically. They brought in reinforcements until Pearse was heavily outnumbered. They strengthened the Castle garrison, isolated the insurgents north of the river from the rest, and – shelling and burning its surroundings – closed slowly in on the Post Office.

Pearse's position was, from the first, a hopeless one, nor did he himself believe that it could be otherwise. The I.R.B. had revolted not to succeed, but to inspire future success. They had deliberately sacrificed themselves in the cause of their freedom.

On the Saturday after Easter when the centre of Dublin lay smouldering in ruin and over a thousand men, women and children were killed and wounded, the members of the Provisional Government of the Irish Republic surrendered. They and other leaders, to the number of sixteen, were executed.

And then a strange thing happened. From being unpopular extremists, these men became heroes; from being unknown, their names became famous. Public opinion in Britain looked upon the rising, with its undertones of German collaboration, as an act of treachery. Public opinion over much of Ireland, quite suddenly, came to see things differently – came to accept the survivors of the revolt as the leaders of a new Ireland. In the streets they sang a new song:

> *It was down the glen, one Easter morn,*
> *To a city fair rode I,*
> *There armed lines of marching men*
> *In squadrons passed me by;*
> *No pipes did hum nor battle drum*
> *Did sound its dread tattoo,*
> *But the Angelus bell o'er the Liffey swell*
> *Rang out in the Foggy Dew.*

> *Right proudly high over Dublin town*
> *They hung out the flag of war,*
> *'Twas better to die 'neath an Irish sky*
> *Than at Suvla or Sedd-el-Bahr;*
> *And from the plains of Royal Meath*
> *Strong men came hurrying through*
> *While Britannia's sons with their great guns*
> *Sailed in through the Foggy Dew.*[10]

NOTES

1 Many different versions of the I.R.B. oath of initiation are on record. See Pollard, H. B. C. *The secret societies of Ireland* Allan, 1922. pp. 56 *et seq.* for the early ones and p. 291 for that said to have been in use in 1914. The version quoted here is based on that given by Peadar O'Cearnaigh, who took the oath in 1903. See de Burca, S. *The soldier's song* Dublin: P. J. Burke, 1957. p. 86.

2 Anonymous. Published by Walton's, Dublin.

3 Redmond, who spoke in the House of Commons on 3 August 1914, is reported in *The parliamentary debates (official report)* Fifth series, vol. LXV, cols. 1828–9.

4 From Editorial by Arthur Griffith in *Sinn Fein*, v, No. 225, 8 August 1914. p. 4.

5 Ryan, D. *The man called Pearse* London & Dublin: Maunsel, 1919. p. 38.

6 The oration is printed in *Souvenir of public funeral to Glasnevin Cemetery, Dublin, 1st August 1915* O'Donovan Rossa Funeral Committee, 1915. p. 35 *et seq.* and also in Pearse, P. H. *Collected works: political writings and speeches* Dublin: Maunsel, 1922. pp. 133 *et seq.*

7 Devoy, J. *Devoy's post bag, 1871–1928*; ed. by W. O'Brien and D. Ryan. 2 vols. Dublin, Fallon, 1948–53. vol. 2, p. 488.

8 *Sunday Independent* 23 April 1916.

9 A reproduction of the 1916 Proclamation appears on p. 111 of this book and on p. 24 of the pupils' pamphlet.

10 Anonymous. Published by Walton's, Dublin. Suvla Bay and Sedd-el-Bahr were the scenes of severe fighting during the unsuccessful allied attempt to enter the Dardanelles and occupy Constantinople in 1915, during the First World War. The heavy casualties included many Irish soldiers of the old regular army and of the Tenth (Irish) Division of Kitchener's new army.

10

THE 'TROUBLES'

G. A. Hayes-McCoy

Summary

MANY IRISHMEN see the Easter rising as merely the first round in an inevitable struggle for independence. The rising has raised passions that cannot be forgotten. Sinn Fein profits from the political upset and becomes republican. It gains strength from the Government's delay in implementing Home Rule and from the threat of conscription.

In the general election of 1918, Sinn Fein sweeps the polls. Sinn Fein sets up a National Assembly (Dail Eireann) in Dublin and ratifies the proclamation of 1916. 'Volunteers' seize gelignite in County Tipperary and kill two policemen. Sinn Fein's reaction is to declare that Crown forces will be treated as an 'invading enemy'.

The situation quickly deteriorates. The police become depleted through mass resignation. Many police stations are blown up. Violence, murder and reprisals become common. The authorities send police reinforcements from Britain ('Black and Tans' and Auxiliaries). By 1921 the casualties amount to three thousand. In July 1921 a truce is signed.

I gave my love a handkerchief,
Red, white and blue,
She gave it to the I.R.A.,
And they tore it up in two,
So right away, right away,
So right away my jolly fine fellows, right away.

And when the war is over,
What will the Tommies do?
They only have a leg and a half,
And the Shinners will have two,
So right away, right away,
So right away my jolly fine fellows, right away.

Never marry a soldier, a sailor or a marine,
But marry a good Sinn Feinner, with his yellow, white or green,
So right away, right away,
So right away my jolly fine fellows, right away.[1]

Whatever way you look at it, the Easter rising of 1916, of which we spoke last week, was an astonishing affair. Short of being an insurgent military success which was impossible, it could not have had a great effect. Brought about by extremists, suppressed with war-time severity, it decided the subsequent course of Anglo-Irish affairs in those last tempestuous years of union – the years before 1922 – a course which was to be marked by stubbornness, suffering, sacrifice, and marked too by increasing violence.

For Britain the Easter revolt was a stab in the back, an outrage that must be met by firm government. On the other hand, an increasing number of Irishmen came to see the rising as merely the first round of an inevitable struggle and resigned themselves to face later ones.

The rising raised issues and aroused passions that could not be forgotten. It scattered hopes of Home Rule and of moderation to the four winds. Sinn Fein profited enormously by the political upset which followed. The Sinn Fein Party, which was founded, as we know, by Arthur Griffith and others in 1905, strove for a self-governing, self-supporting, industrialized Ireland. It believed that this ideal state might be attained if the Irish people organized in their own interest and if their elected representatives ignored, and abstained from attending the Union Parliament in Westminster.

This goal and this policy remained the same as the years went by, but in the changes that followed the 1916 rising the Sinn Feiners became republicans. They wanted Ireland to be ruled by an Irish parliament elected by the Irish people. They became too the leaders of a new Ireland. By 1918 these 'Shinners', as the British called them, working in co-operation with the reorganized Irish Volunteers, had already gained much ground. A great deal of their new strength came from the Government's decision to execute the 1916 leaders, so making them political martyrs in Ireland. They gained too from the forceful leadership of those who had survived the 1916 rising and from the mounting disillusionment of the people at the Government's delay in granting the long-promised Home Rule. Most of all, they gained from the threat of Britain, which was still fighting for its life against Germany, to enforce military conscription:

Will you join the forces as free men, able to choose your unit in the Army, Navy or Air Force, or will you wait till you have to join, and have no choice as to where you are sent? Will you give us your quota, or must three times as many be taken under compulsion?[2]

In response to such words as these the Irish showed themselves to be a proud people, and as well as that a distinct people, with an outlook of their own. They listened to the call of the Volunteer leaders and they joined the Irish Volunteers.

The government of a foreign nation, occupying our country by force of arms, not content with its usual plundering and oppression, now proposes to inflict upon you the manhood of Ireland, a fate worse than death. It claims power, not only over your lives, but over your souls; it dares to threaten us not merely with death – for which we have shown how little we care – but the most degraded of deaths: to die fighting as the slaves for our enemies in a fight, that is not ours!

In this emergency every true Volunteer should know how to act for himself; it is his duty to resist conscription to the death. Don't argue – shoot![3]

But in November 1918 the Great War came to an end and the threat to conscript Irishmen into the British forces was never carried out. Great numbers of young men who had joined the Irish Volunteers in the hope of saving themselves from service in the British forces soon fell away. But the rebels in the volunteer ranks remained to back Sinn Fein in the struggle for separation from Britain.

Then in December 1918 a general election was held. When the

votes were counted the Parliamentary Party, the champions of Home Rule and the former leaders of Ireland, held only 6 seats. The Unionists won 26, 23 of which were in the province of Ulster. The rest fell to Sinn Fein – 73 seats out of 105. They had swept the country.

Half of these Sinn Fein members of parliament were in prison. The Government had arrested them as they said:

For encouraging and aiding persons to commit crime, for inciting persons to acts of violence and intimidation, and for interfering with the administration of the law.[4]

But the Sinn Fein members who were still at liberty set up a National Assembly in Dublin or, as they called it in the Irish language, Dail Éireann.

The Dail met in January 1919. Both Unionists and Home Rule members were invited to attend, but they refused to do so. Sinn Fein, accepting leadership and taking advantage of their victory, set up what was intended to be an Irish national government and adopted a declaration of independence.

The Irish people is by right a free people. And whereas English rule in this country is and always has been based upon force and fraud and maintained by military occupation against the declared will of the people; and whereas the Irish Republic was proclaimed in Dublin on Easter Monday, 1916, by the Irish Republican Army acting on behalf of the Irish people; and whereas the Irish electorate has, in the General Election of December 1918 declared by an overwhelming majority its firm allegiance to the Irish Republic.

Now therefore, we ratify the establishment of the Irish Republic and pledge ourselves and our people to make this declaration effective by every means at our command. . .

In the name of the Irish people we humbly commit our destiny to Almighty God. We ask His Divine blessing on this the last stage of the struggle which we have pledged ourselves to carry through to Freedom. . .[5]

Extra! Extra! Evening paper. Special extra. Two policemen shot dead. Two policemen shot dead in Tipperary. Extra! Extra!. . .

The Troubles had begun. On 21 January 1919, the very day on which Dail Eireann adopted the declaration of the Irish Republic, a group of Volunteers seized a cart-load of gelignite at Soloheadbeg, County Tipperary. Two policemen who were guarding the gelignite and who tried to stop them were shot dead.

There had, of course, been much aggression on the part of the British Government before this – baton charges, raids, arrests and deportations by the hundred; but the shooting in Tipperary and the attitude in regard to it promptly taken up by Irish Volunteer headquarters indicated a new departure. Said the Volunteers:

The Irish Government claims the same power and authority as any other lawfully constituted government. It sanctions the employment by the Irish Volunteers of the most drastic measures against the enemies of Ireland. The soldiers and police of the invader are liable to be treated exactly as invading enemy soldiers would be treated by the native army of any country.

Every Volunteer is entitled, morally and legally, when in the execution of his military duties, to use all legitimate means of warfare against them, and to slay them if it is necessary to do so in order to overcome their resistance. England must be given the choice between evacuating this country and holding it by a foreign garrison in a perpetual state of war. [6]

Amid growing tension, mounting anxiety, heightened tragedy – at a time when Europe after her four years' struggle was seeking again the ways of peace – the guns were out once more in Ireland. This time Ireland was to see a new kind of warfare, a warfare that was directed primarily against the force which, according to the Volunteers, Britain was using to maintain her grip on the country, the Royal Irish Constabulary.

One by one, in Cork, Clare, Limerick, Tipperary, Meath, Monaghan, and soon in other counties as well, the police barracks were attacked. Many fell. Many were burnt. Many were blown up. Others held out heroically. But by the summer of 1920 the result was clear: the Volunteers had increased their stock of arms – almost every rifle, every revolver, every round of ammunition that they had was captured from their opponents and over wide areas the authority of the police had declined. They admitted it:

There is hostility to the police everywhere, and through a great part of the country I do not regard it as safe for a single police vehicle to travel.

We are losing men every day from retirements and resignations and getting practically no recruits. I see no alternative to evacuating some of the stations that we still hold. At present we run the risk of being weak everywhere and strong nowhere. [7]

Smaller barracks were abandoned. In two nights' work – what a boost for the morale of the Volunteers! – over three hundred of them were destroyed. The eyes of the British administration were being blinded and its ears stopped up. And – perhaps inevitably – the struggle soon assumed a more terrible aspect.

One night in March 1920 the Lord Mayor of Cork was killed. The jury at the inquest returned a unanimous verdict:

We find that the late Alderman MacCurtain, Lord Mayor of Cork, died from shock and haemorrhage caused by bullet wounds, and that he was wilfully murdered under circumstances of the most callous brutality, and that the murder was organised and carried out by the Royal Irish Constabulary, officially directed by the British Government, and we return a verdict of wilful murder against David Lloyd George, Prime Minister of England; Lord French, Lord Lieutenant of Ireland; Ian MacPherson, late Chief Secretary of Ireland; Acting Inspector General Smith, of the Royal Irish Constabulary. . .[8]

Thomas MacCurtain was killed because, in addition to being Lord Mayor of Cork, he was Commandant of Cork No. 1 Brigade of the Irish Volunteers. The ten thousand people who in a shuttered city walked in his funeral procession saw nothing odd in his holding at one time the two posts.

Lord French, who was then supreme governor of Ireland, had been appointed to *his* post because he was a distinguished British soldier. Military and civil affairs were, in the situation which had by that time developed, hopelessly mixed up – on both sides. Violence, which was a soldier's trade, not a Lord Lieutenant's or a Lord Mayor's, had corrupted everything.

But unlike the insurrection of 1916 the Volunteers made no attempt to establish formal open control of key positions. Instead, they aimed at striking swift and repeated blows at the British administration in Ireland, emerging from and disappearing into the civilian population.

The strength of the contestants was quite out of proportion – 40,000 soldiers and policemen against, at most, 3,000 armed Volunteers – yet Britain sent in reinforcements. The British Government was under constant criticism in Parliament and in the world press. And so in keeping with the claim that the fighting in Ireland was not war but civil disorder, it was most notably the police, rather than the military, who were reinforced. And since sufficient Irish police recruits could no longer be obtained the required strength was made up by British ones.

In March 1920 the first of the police reinforcements arrived. They were nicknamed the Black and Tans, and they were followed in July by the Auxiliaries. A British spokesman made their mission clear:

They did not wait for the usual uniform, these Black and Tans who have joined the R.I.C. They came at once. They know what danger is. They have looked death in the eyes before and did not flinch. They will not flinch now. They will go on with the job – the job of making Ireland once again safe for the law-abiding, and an appropriate hell for those whose trade is agitation, and whose method is murder.[9]

The terror reached its height in the winter of 1920. In those dark days Michael Collins was the outstanding leader of the revolt. In the grim battles of the Dublin shadows, each gloomy morning brought gloomier news – of raids, shootings and ambushes, and of the organized reprisals that followed them, the burning of creameries and the sacking of towns. Curfew, hunger strikes, the shooting of civilians and the wrecking of homes made a savage background to the everyday life of a people who wished passionately that it could all be over – but whose hearts hardened increasingly towards Britain.

> *In Mountjoy Jail, one Monday morning,*
> *High upon the gallows tree,*
> *Kevin Barry gave his young life,*
> *For the cause of liberty.*
>
> *But a lad of eighteen summers,*
> *Yet no one can deny,*
> *As he walked to death that morning,*
> *He proudly held his head on high.*
>
> *Another martyr for old Ireland,*
> *Another murder for the Crown,*
> *Whose brutal laws may kill the Irish,*
> *But cannot keep their spirit down.*

Despite the many successes of the Volunteers, who developed in those still early days of mechanical transport, a new kind of guerrilla warfare and whose flying columns became expert in the tactics of ambushing their lorry-borne enemies, the military defeat of Britain was, of course, impossible. The object of the Volunteers had been to make British rule in Ireland impossible and they had succeeded. The British Government had to come to terms or else undertake a full-scale military conquest in order, as a British

General put it, 'to flatten the rebels'. Few people in Britain would have countenanced such an undertaking.

By 1921, as the list of killed and wounded in this extraordinary war mounted to three thousand, Englishmen became angry with their government which had chosen to ignore the expressed desire of the majority of Irish people for independence. One such was the writer, Sir Philip Gibbs, who said:

I condemn the warfare of ambush and assassination waged by the Sinn Fein extremists. I think it is evil and disastrous. I have great pity for those men of the R.I.C. shot down coldly often without a dog's chance of self-defence, and I sicken at the constant record of young English soldiers killed in this miserable vendetta. But our regulars and auxiliaries and Black and Tans ought not to be in Ireland to be shot at in this way. It is due to the hard, bitter stupidity of English statesmen and officials that they are there at all – to men who would rather see Ireland drenched in blood than grant the Irish a single generous concession or come to any kind of terms with their acknowledged leaders.[11]

Yet it had been a war between two more or less independent military authorities. On one side the Dail did not always exercise full control over the activities of the Volunteers and on the other the Black and Tans and Auxiliaries were not effectively disciplined by the Crown. In the end a spirit of generous concession did prevail.

A truce was negotiated in July 1921 and – after discussion between British and Irish representatives – a treaty was signed in December. These were the words of Arthur Griffith, the first President of the resulting Irish Free State:

I believe this treaty will lay the foundations of peace and friendship between the two nations. What I have signed I shall stand by in the belief that the end of the conflict of centuries is at hand.[12]

NOTES

1 Anonymous.

2 From a recruiting poster of 1918 quoted in Beasley, P. *Michael Collins and the making of a new Ireland* 2 vols. Harrap, 1926. vol. 1, p. 229.

3 *An tÓglách:* official organ of the Irish Volunteers, I, No. 2, 14 September 1918.

4 Proclamation by Lord Lieutenant and Privy Council in Ireland, printed in *The Freeman's Journal* 4 July 1918. p. 3.

5 *Declaration of Independence, message to the free nations and democratic pro-gramme adopted by Dail Eireann, 21 January 1919* Quoted in Curtis, E. and McDowell, R. B., eds. *Irish historical documents, 1171–1922* Methuen, 1943.

6 These passages are quoted from official Irish Volunteer statements appearing in *An tÓglách*, I, Nos 10 and 11, 31 January 1919 and February 1919.

7 Reports of County Inspectors of R.I.C. in Waterford and Kerry, with comments of Divisional Commissioner, August 1920 captured at the time by the Irish Volunteers and printed in Beasley, P. *Michael Collins and the making of a new Ireland* op. cit. vol. 2, pp. 43 *et seq.*

8 The verdict and full report of the Coroner's inquest, 20 March to 17 April 1920, are printed in O'Donoghue, F. *Tomás MacCurtain* Tralee: Kerryman, 1958. pp. 167 *et seq.*

9 Quoted from *The Weekly Summary* an official police news-sheet, August 1920.

10 Anonymous.

11 Philip Gibbs in preface to Martin, H. *Ireland in insurrection* D. O'Connor, 1921. pp. 17 *et seq.*

12 Original statement signed by Arthur Griffith, in National Museum of Ireland, Dublin.

I I

NORTHERN IRELAND

Martin Wallace

Summary

IN 1920, the Government of Ireland Act sets up two Irish parliaments, one in Belfast to govern the six north-eastern counties, and the other in Dublin. The Unionists accept the Act, but the rest of Ireland rejects it and renewed fighting leads to an 'Irish Free State' covering twenty-six counties. Eamon de Valera and his Republican supporters repudiate the settlement but are defeated, in a civil war.

The new government in 'Northern Ireland' is faced with recurring tension between the Protestant majority and the Roman

Catholic minority in the six counties, and the illegal Irish Republican Army engages in sporadic terrorism. Northern Ireland plays an important part in the Second World War, and the Ireland Act of 1949 reinforces its status within the United Kingom.

In the 1960s, there is resistance to attempts to improve relations between Protestants and Catholics, and eventually widespread civil disturbances lead to a resurgence of the I.R.A. and the suspension of the Northern Ireland Parliament and Government. Amid continuing violence, Ulster's longstanding problems are subjected to close scrutiny, and a system of power-sharing is developed so that Protestant and Catholic politicians can join for the first time in governing the province.

I N 1920, the British Government made a new attempt to solve the Irish problem by passing the Government of Ireland Act. This Act set up two Irish Parliaments, one in Belfast to govern the six north-eastern counties and one in Dublin to govern the other twenty-six counties.

The Parliament of what was called 'Northern Ireland' met for the first time in June 1921. The opening ceremony was carried out by King George V, who said:

I speak from a full heart when I pray that my coming to Ireland today may prove to be the first step towards an end of strife amongst her people, whatever their race or creed. I appeal to all Irishmen to forgive and forget and to join in making for the land they love a new era of peace, contentment and goodwill.[1]

The King's hopes were not fulfilled. The rest of Ireland was unwilling to accept the 1920 Act, and bitter fighting continued until July 1921, when a truce was arranged. In December 1921, British and Irish representatives signed what is usually called the Anglo-Irish Treaty, which provided for an 'Irish Free State'. Northern Ireland was given the choice of remaining within the United Kingdom, and the Northern Parliament immediately voted to take this course.

Many of the Southern Irish were unhappy with the treaty, which required that members of the Free State Parliament should take an oath of allegiance to the British crown. De Valera had not signed the treaty, and Southern Ireland gradually drifted into a bitter civil war between the 'Free Staters', led by Arthur Griffith and Michael Collins, and the 'Republicans', led by De Valera. By the time the Free Staters won victory in May 1923, Collins had been killed in an ambush and Griffith had died of exhaustion.

The 1921 treaty had provided that, if Northern Ireland voted itself out of the Irish Free State, a Boundary Commission should be set up to decide where the border should be drawn between the two parts of Ireland, according to the wishes of the inhabitants. Collins had believed that its findings would lead to a united Ireland.

We would save Tyrone and Fermanagh, parts of Derry, Armagh and Down by the Boundary Commission; the North would be forced economically to come in.[2]

But Sir James Craig, Northern Ireland's first Prime Minister, was determined to give away 'not an inch' of the six counties, and refused to nominate an Ulster member of the commission. In spite of this, the commission was formed in November 1924, but its work came to a halt a year later when a London newspaper, the *Morning Post*, published a fairly accurate account of the commission's draft proposals.

The newspaper report showed that the commission had no intention of giving Fermanagh and Tyrone, counties with a Roman Catholic majority, to the Free State. Instead, part of east Donegal, where there were many Protestant farmers, was to come into Northern Ireland. Public opinion in the Free State forced the Southern member of the commission, Professor Eoin MacNeill, to resign. Soon afterwards, in December 1925, it was agreed by the governments in London, Dublin and Belfast that Northern Ireland should remain as it was – the six counties of Antrim, Down, Armagh, Fermanagh, Tyrone and Londonderry.

Sir Winston Churchill, then Chancellor of the Exchequer, was among those who signed the 1925 agreement, and he later summed up his views of the border problem in a book about the First World War.

The whole map of Europe has been changed. The position of countries has been violently altered. But as the deluge subsides and the waters fall we see the dreary steeples of Fermanagh and Tyrone emerging once again. The integrity of their quarrel is one of the few institutions that have been unaltered in the cataclysm which has swept the world.[3]

In other words, dividing Ireland into two parts – Partition, as it is commonly called – still left a good many problems unsolved. In Northern Ireland, there was bitterness between Protestants and Roman Catholics which would lead on occasions to rioting and other violence. The predominantly Catholic Free State never became reconciled to Partition, and in 1937 De Valera (now in power by democratic vote) introduced a new constitution which claimed the whole of Ireland as 'the national territory'.

But, despite the problems, successive British governments persevered with the experiment of having a regional parliament in Belfast, and were largely content to let the Unionist administration get on with administering the occasionally unruly province. The major decisions in such matters as defence, foreign policy and income tax were still taken in London, and many of the laws passed at Stormont (the new parliament building on the outskirts of Belfast) were similar to laws passed at Westminster. Northern Ireland still sent members of Parliament to Westminster – but only twelve, eventually, compared with thirty before Partition.

The system of having a local parliament is called *devolution*, because the main parliament devolves or hands over some of its powers. In 1938, Sir David Keir summed up the good and bad points of the Ulster experiment.

The Northern administration has on the whole justified the belief that devolution would lead to greater efficiency. This has been specially evident in agriculture and education, but it is otherwise on the political side. The special circumstances of the North-East have not produced and cannot produce a healthy alternation of parties in power. The Protestant majority have monopolized government since 1920. New Parties have been stifled.[4]

In 1922, the Unionist government abolished the system of proportional representation in voting for local councils. The system was designed to ensure fair representation for minority parties, but the Unionists proceeded to re-draw electoral boundaries so as to gain control of some councils (notably Londonderry) previously controlled by Nationalists.

In 1929, they abolished proportional representation in the Northern Ireland Parliament, largely to ensure that Protestants would vote solidly for the Unionist Party and not support breakaway groups. Although Nationalists complained that the new constituencies had been gerrymandered – that is, drawn to give Unionist candidates the best chance of winning – the membership of Parliament scarcely changed, as Denis Barritt and Charles Carter pointed out in 1962.

> Our general conclusion is that in its composition the Northern Ireland Parliament reflects the views of the people with no more distortion than is normally to be found in democratic parliaments. Its real peculiarity is that it has no alternation of parties in office.[5]

Craig, who later became Lord Craigavon, was a man of greater tolerance and vision than many of his supporters. He chose a Roman Catholic as chief civil servant in the Ministry of Education, and arranged financial help for Catholic schools. Another Catholic became Lord Chief Justice.

But in its struggle to maintain peace, the Northern Ireland Government recruited a predominantly Protestant force, the so-called 'B' Specials, to assist the regular police, the Royal Ulster Constabulary. Under successive Special Powers Acts, the government took wide powers to deal with terrorism, and suspects could be arrested without warrant and interned without trial.

Roman Catholics felt that their community suffered heavily from such measures, and that they were generally treated less fairly than Protestants. Lord Craigavon sometimes made speeches aimed at appeasing his anti-Catholic supporters.

> I have always said I am an Orangeman first and a politician and member of this parliament afterwards . . . all I boast is that we are a Protestant parliament and a Protestant state.[6]

When Craigavon died in 1940, the Second World War was in progress. Northern Ireland, as part of the United Kingdom, stood alongside Great Britain in her struggle for survival. Since the Irish Free State remained neutral, Northern Ireland was of great strategic importance, and the port of Londonderry became a major base for British and American ships in the battle against German submarines. Sir Winston Churchill paid tribute to the protection given to incoming ships.

> All had to come in around Northern Ireland. Here, by the grace of God, Ulster stood a faithful sentinel. The Mersey, the Clyde were the lungs through which we breathed.[7]

The war brought new jobs to Northern Ireland, which had been economically depressed during the 1920s and 1930s. This eased the religious tension, as did the shared experience of bombing raids on Belfast. After the war, the benefits of the British welfare state raised living standards noticeably above those in the Free State.

In 1948, the Free State Government decided to sever its links with the British Commonwealth, and the Republic of Ireland formally came into being the following year. Also in 1949, Westminster passed the Ireland Act, declaring that Northern Ireland would not cease to be part of the United Kingdom 'without the consent of the Parliament of Northern Ireland'.

In 1956, the illegal Irish Republican Army opened a new campaign of violence in Northern Ireland, attacking army barracks, customs posts and other symbols of the 'British occupation'. The government at Stormont revived its powers under the Special Powers Act, and the campaign petered out in 1962. The Catholic population gave little support to the I.R.A. terrorists, and there were no clashes between Ulster's two religious communities.

In 1963, Captain Terence O'Neill became Ulster's Prime Minister, replacing the ageing Lord Brookeborough, who had held office for twenty years. O'Neill spoke of 'building bridges in the community', for he believed that Northern Ireland could only achieve full peace and prosperity it if commanded the support and efforts of all its citizens.

He also sought better relations between the two parts of Ireland, and in January 1965 welcomed the Prime Minister of the Republic, Sean Lemass, on a visit to Stormont. It was an historic occasion, the first such meeting for forty years, but O'Neill began to lose the support of some Protestants who distrusted Catholics and feared that his policies would lead to a united Ireland.

O'Neill's principal critic was Rev. Ian Paisley, leader of the breakaway Free Presbyterian Church, who also opposed the worldwide ecumenical movement which was drawing the different Christian Churches closer together. In 1966, Protestant anger increased as Republicans celebrated the fiftieth anniversary of the 1916 Easter Rising on a large scale, and there were clashes involving police and both Protestant and Catholic mobs.

A Protestant terrorist organization, the Ulster Volunteer Force, emerged and was declared illegal. The murder of two Catholics was attributed to the U.V.F., and these were to prove the forerunners of many other sectarian killings in the 1970s.

O'Neill's leadership of the Unionist Party was increasingly challenged from within the Protestant community, but he held to his policies of moderation and tolerance. Unfortunately, the pace of his reforms did not satisfy the Catholic community, whose hopes had been aroused, and by 1968 he was under pressure from a strong civil rights movement which produced new Catholic leaders.

The movement criticised local councils for discriminating against Roman Catholics in employment and in the allocation of council houses. It complained of gerrymandering and sought 'one man, one vote' in local government elections – in other words, universal franchise as in parliamentary elections, rather than a vote restricted to rate-payers, their spouses and business companies.

In October 1968, the Government banned a proposed civil rights march in Londonderry. The march went ahead, and there was a clash with the police, who were widely criticized for using batons to disperse the large crowd.

O'Neill, now under pressure also from a concerned British Government, promised more reforms. But the violence steadily worsened, and – as he put it in a broadcast to the people – Ulster stood 'at the crossroads'.

What kind of Ulster do you want? A happy and respected province in good standing with the rest of the United Kingdom? Or a place continually torn apart by riots and demonstrations, and regarded by the rest of Britain as a political outcast?[8]

In February 1969, O'Neill called a sudden general election in the hope of winning clear public support for his policies. The result was inconclusive, for most of his critics within the Unionist Parliamentary Party retained their seats at Stormont, and in April O'Neill resigned.

His successor, Major James Chichester-Clark, faced a deteriorating situation, with frequent rioting and clashes between Protestant and Catholic demonstrators. A critical clash came in Londonderry in August 1969, when Catholic youths stoned the annual march of Apprentice Boys (old men as well as young) celebrating the siege of the city in 1689, when thirteen Protestant apprentices had closed the gates against James II's army.

As police sought to control the rioters, who retreated behind barricades into the Catholic Bogside district of Londonderry, there followed disturbances in other Ulster towns and many attacks on police stations. After two days, troops moved into Londonderry to restore peace, and a day later into Belfast. By this time, several people had been killed in the Belfast riots, and a tribunal of inquiry later commented on police behaviour in the city.

The Tribunal finds that the R.U.C. are to be criticized for their failure to disperse mobs or protect lives and property on 15 August during the hours of daylight before the arrival of the army.[9]

The years since then have seen the re-emergence of the I.R.A., at first claiming the role of protectors of the Catholic communities against Protestant mobs (though the troops were committed to this task) and then embarking on a campaign of bombing and killing designed to destroy the economic life of Northern Ireland and bring about an all-Ireland republic.

Protestant militancy has grown in response, with intimidation and killing of Catholics commonplace. Within five years of the 1969 riots, more than one thousand soldiers, policemen and civilians had been killed.

Major Chichester-Clark instituted substantial reforms after discussions with the British Government. The R.U.C. was re-organised and the 'B' Specials replaced by a part-time Ulster Defence Regiment under army control. Measures were taken to curb religious discrimination in housing and employment.

However, Chichester-Clark came under much the same sort of Protestant pressure as O'Neill had felt, and he resigned in March 1971. His successor, Brian Faulkner, introduced internment in August 1971 only to see the violence increase.

In March 1972, the British Government suspended the Ulster Parliament and a Secretary of State for Northern Ireland, William Whitelaw, took over responsibility for governing the province. This period of 'direct rule' lasted until the beginning of 1974, when a new Northern Ireland Executive took office.

By this time, following negotiations at Sunningdale in England, in which the Dublin government also took part, the old parliament had been replaced by an Assembly elected by proportional representation. The new executive was a "power-sharing" coalition of Unionists led by Faulkner, the Chief Executive, the largely Catholic Social Democratic and Labour Party (which had supplanted the Nationalists) and the moderate new Alliance Party.

The British Government retained responsibility for security matters, including the police and the courts, and replaced the

Special Powers Acts with legislation providing greater safeguards for those held without trial. There were proposals for a Council of Ireland, first envisaged in the 1920 Act, which would bring North and South closer together.

As this new attempt to solve the Irish question got under way, the I.R.A. remained on the offensive and there was strong Protestant opposition to the Sunningdale proposals and particularly to the Council of Ireland. In May 1974, a general strike was called by the Protestant Ulster Workers' Council, and its success led to the executive's resignation. Direct rule was reinstituted, and the British Government made plans to replace the Assembly with an elected Constitutional Convention in which Ulster people could make a new attempt to resolve the province's problems. Ulster remained at the crossroads.

NOTES

1 Quoted in Shearman, H. F. *Not an inch: a study of Northern Ireland and Lord Craigavon* Faber, 1942. p. 159.

2 In a memorandum quoted by Hyde, H. M. in an article in *Belfast Telegraph* 6 December 1960.

3 Churchill, W. S. *The world crisis: the aftermath* Thornton Butterworth, 1929. p. 319.

4 Keir, Sir D. L. *The constitutional history of modern Britain, 1485–1937* Black, 1938, p. 525.

5 Barritt, D. P. and Carter, C. F. *The Northern Ireland problem: a study in group relations* O.U.P., 1962. p. 43.

6 Speech in the Northern Ireland House of Commons, 24 April 1934.

7 Quoted in Falls, C. *Northern Ireland and the defence of the British Isles* p. 83 in Wilson, T. ed. *Ulster under home rule* O.U.P., 1955.

8 Broadcast on 9 December 1968.

9 *Violence and civil disturbances in Northern Ireland in 1969; report of tribunal of inquiry* H.M.S.O., 1972. p. 194.

INDEX

Act of Disestablishment (1869), 9 (1871), 95

Act of Union (1800), 35, 36, 37–8, 39, 42

Agitator, The, see O'Connell, Daniel

Agriculture, 5, 6, 10, 12, 23, 84. See also Famine, Landlords, Peasantry

Allen, Fenian, 90

American Civil War
  effect of, on trade, 54, 58
  Irish Americans in, 86, 87–8

Andrews, Thomas, 99

Anglo-Irish Treaty, 18–19, 123, 124

Antrim, County
  insurrection in, 28, 33–4
  Potato Famine in, 46
  Industrial Revolution in, 58

Armagh, County, Potato Famine in, 46
  linen-weaving in, 57
  trade route to, 75

Asquith, H. H., 95, 102

Auxiliaries, British, 114, 120–1

Avondale, County Wicklow, 80

Ballinrobe, 50

Ballymoney, 55

Ballynahinch, 34

Banbridge, 26

Bangor, 55

Bantry Bay, 32

Barritt, Denis, 126

Belfast
  comparisons with Dublin, 5, 11, 22
  population of, 11, 22, 58
  trade expands in, 12, 22, 56–8, 75–6
  Wolfe Tone in, 30
  O'Connell in, 42
  typhus fever in, 51
  Randolph Churchill in, 97
  riots in, 98
  Carson in, 100
  Winston Churchill in, 102

Belfast Newsletter, 31, 58

Belfast Ropework Company, 11

Bernstoff, Count von, 110

Bessbrook, 58

Biggar, Joseph Gillis, 81

Black and Tans, 18, 119, 121

Boer War, Irish Brigades against Britain in, 87, 92

Bonaparte, Napoleon, 8, 32

Bonar Law, Andrew, 100

Boundary Commission (1924), 124

Boycott, Captain, 82

Boyne, Battle of the, 54

Brookeborough, Lord, 127

'B' Specials, 126, 129

'Buckshot', see Forster, W. E.

Butt, Isaac, 13, 78

Canada, emigration to, 45, 52
  invaded by Fenians, 86, 90

Carnot, French War Minister, 32

Carrickfergus, 54

Carson, Sir Edward
  opposes Home Rule, 14, 95, 99–100
  verses on, 96
  as orator, 99
  in Belfast, 100
  meets Redmond in London, 103

Carter, Charles, 126

Casement, Sir Roger, 16, 105, 110

Castlewellan, 58

Catholics, 8, 16, 125
  emancipation of, 8–9
  penal laws against, 19, 20–1, 24
  against Protestants, 19, 20–1, 25–6, 28, 31, 42, 97, 98, 122–3, 125–6, 127–9
  as early inhabitants, 20
  vote given to, 24
  forced to support Church of Ireland, 29
  poverty of, 36
  Parnell's resignation demanded by, 83
  Fenians denounced by, 89
  majority in Nationalist Party, 127
  see also Catholic Association

Catholic Association, 37, 40

Cavan, Lord, 35

French, Lord, 119
Friends, Society of, give aid during Famine, 51

Stockton - Billingham
LIBRARY
Technical College